I0473578

Tranquility

Designs to Inspire Your Creative Genius

Published in 2015 by Global Insight Productions

Illustrations by Tracee Clayton Garret
Creative Director Rosa MeChel

www.BeHappyColoringBooks.com

2015 Copyright belongs to Global Insight Productions. All rights reserved.
No part of this book may be reproduced or transmitted in any form or by
any means, including but not limited to information storage and retrieval
systems, electronic, mechanical, photocopy, recording, etc., without
written permission from the copyright holder.

ISBN: 978-0-9796942-8-8

Join Our Creative Community
BeHappyColoringBooks.com

For your coloring and painting pleasure,
if you have creative genius ideas that you
would like for our artist to design, let us know.

We also want you to be a part of our Be Happy
Art Gallery. So go ahead and send us your
masterpiece and we will share it with the world.

You can contact us at **info@behappycoloring.com**

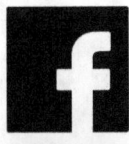 facebook.com/behappycoloring

 pinterest.com/behappycoloring

 Instagram.com/behappycoloring

 twitter.com/behappycoloring

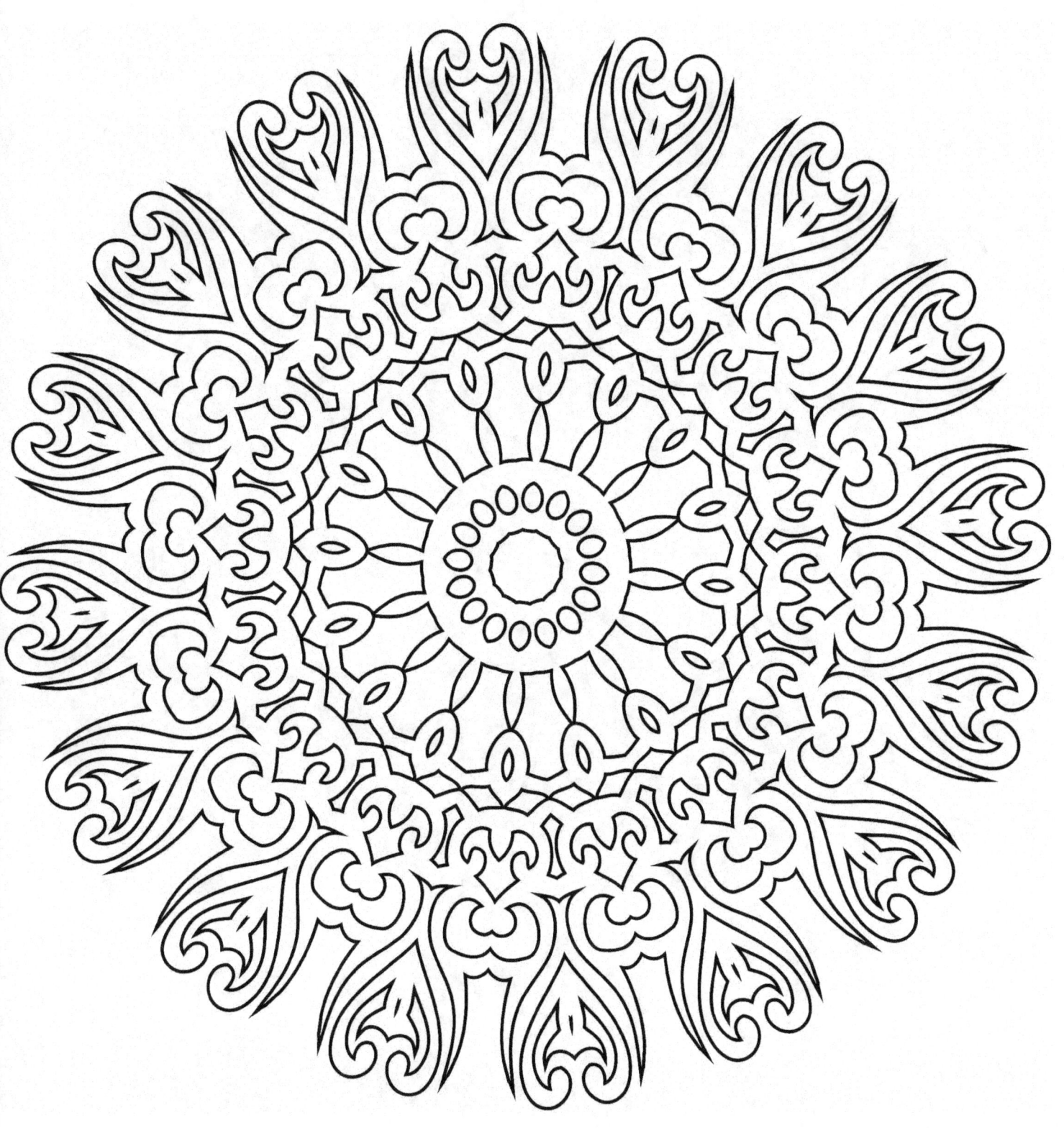

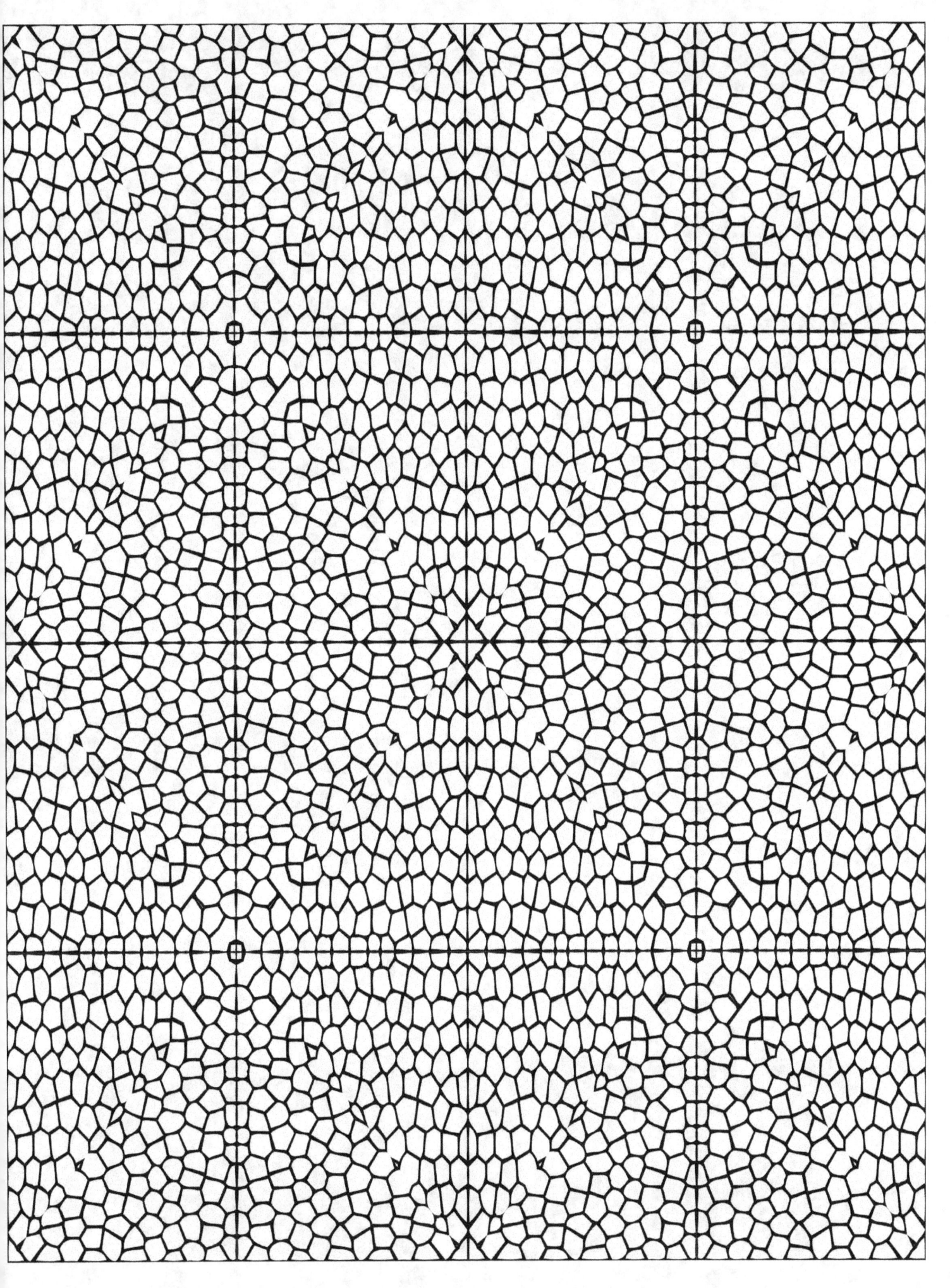

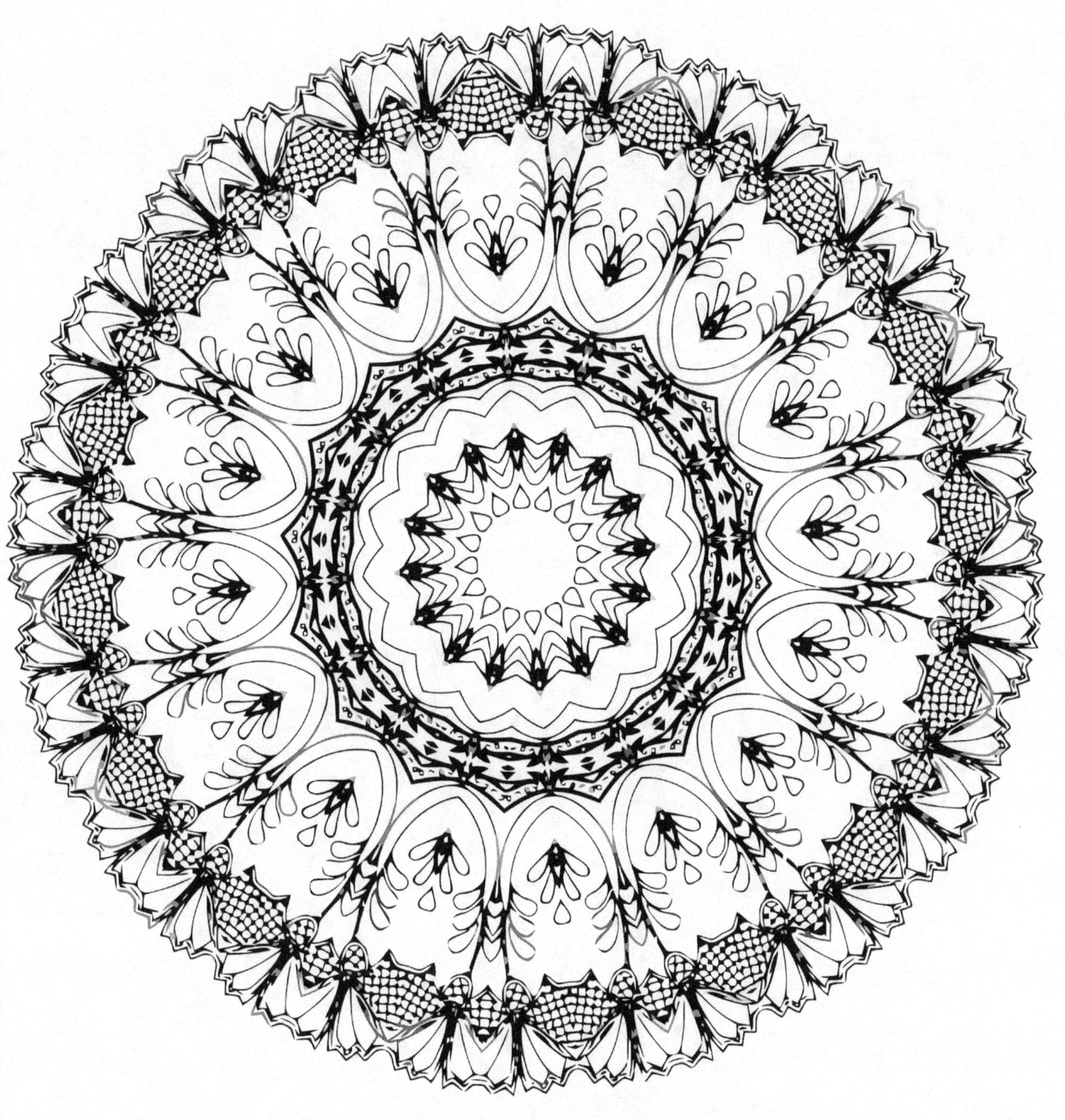

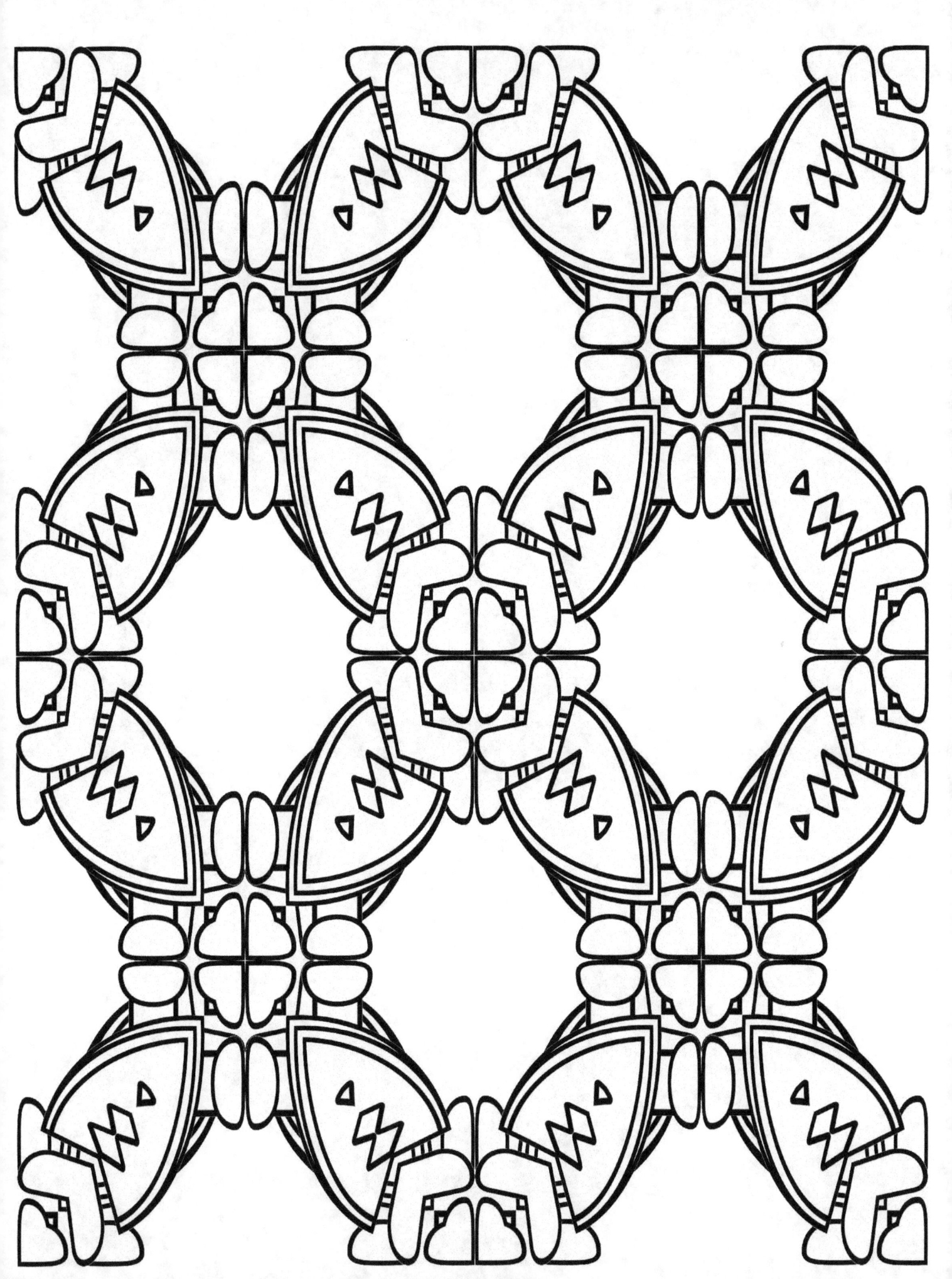

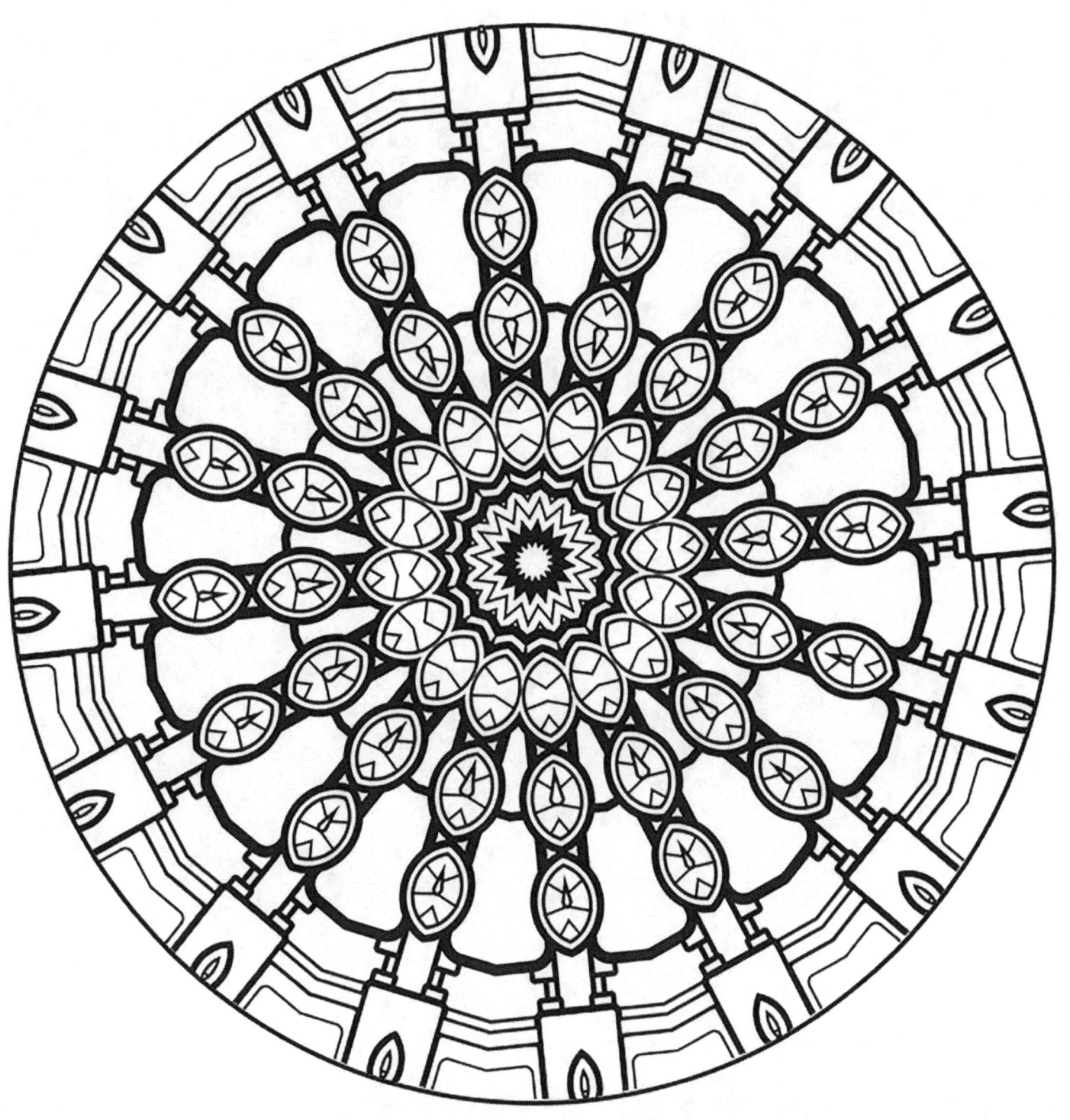

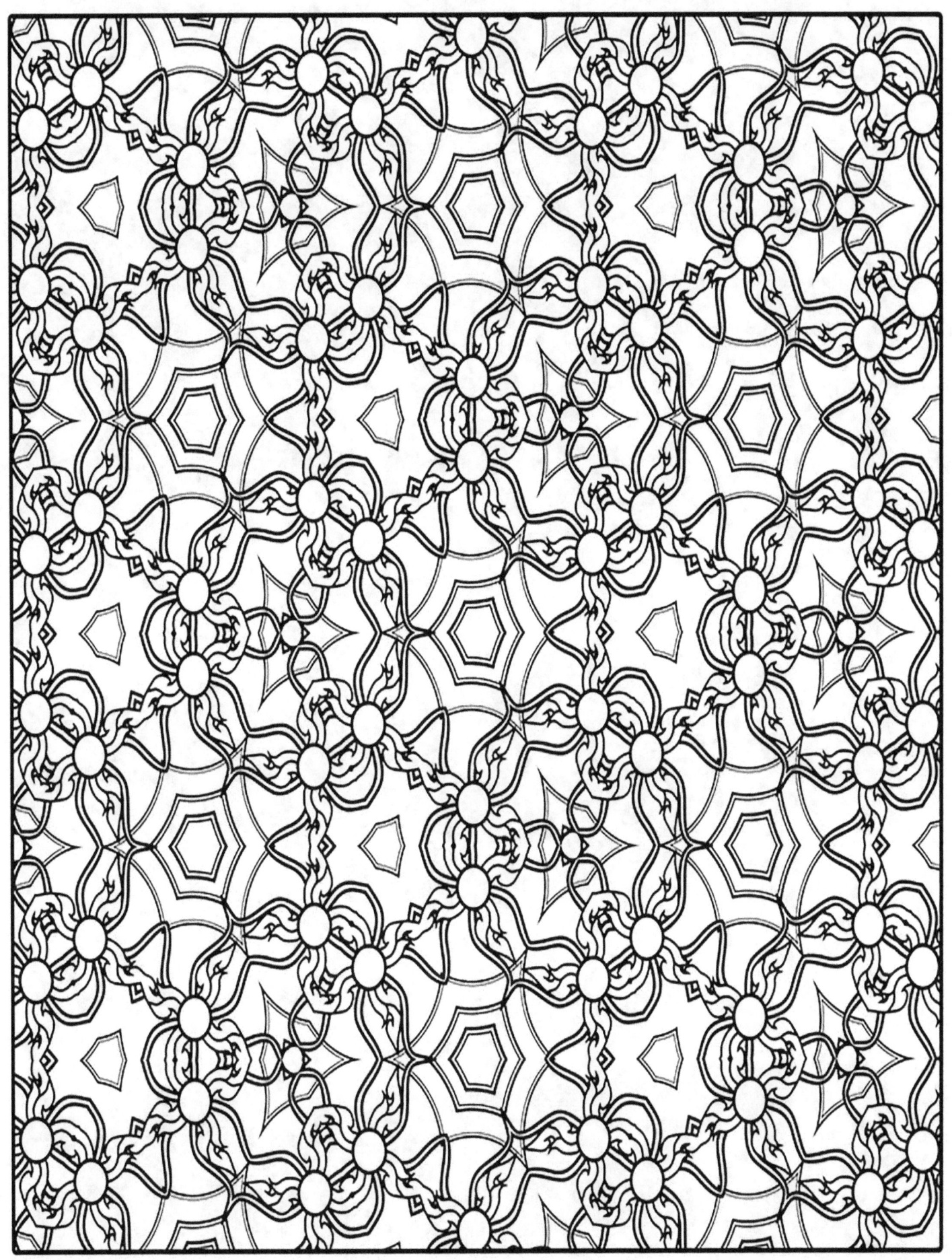

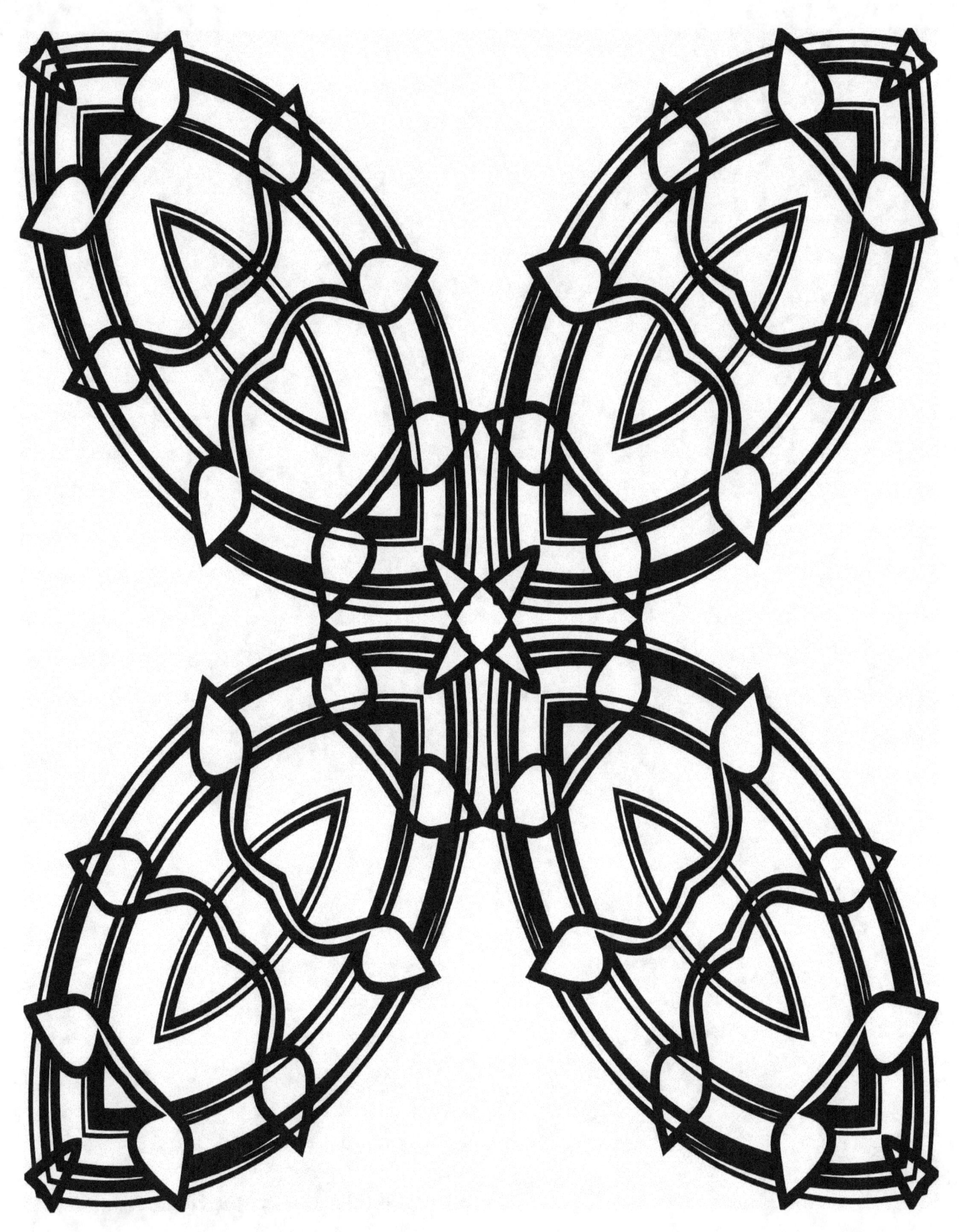

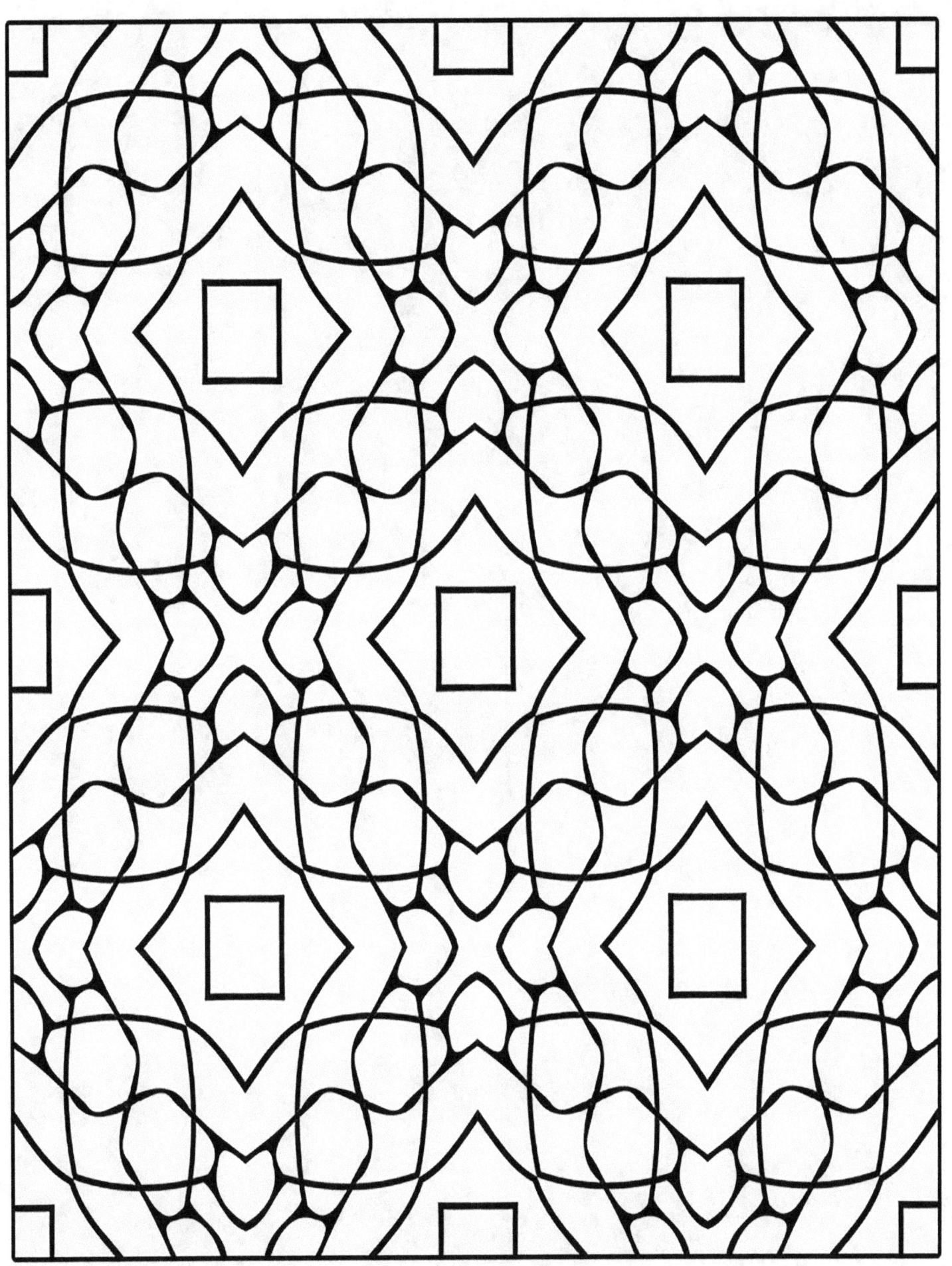

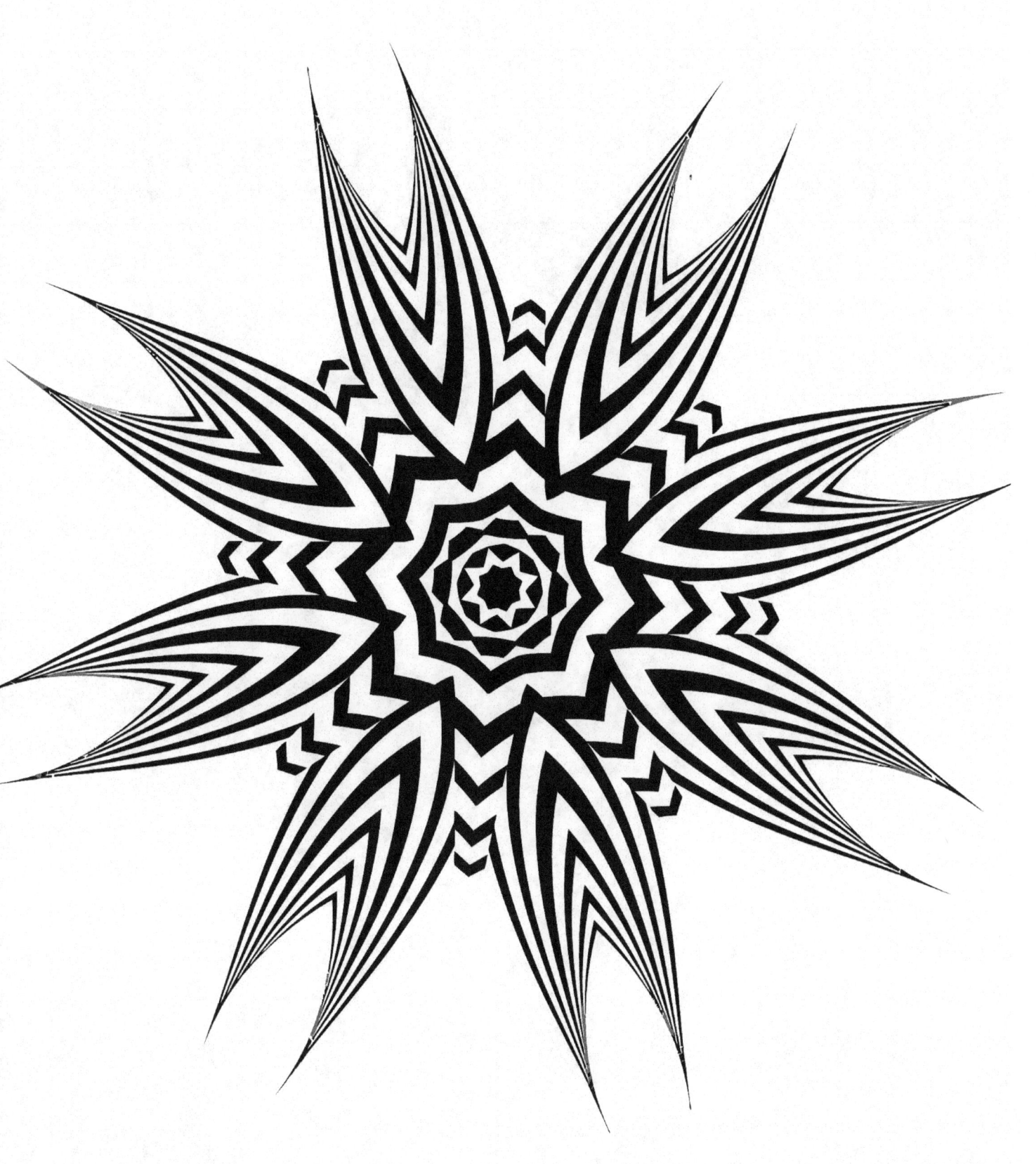

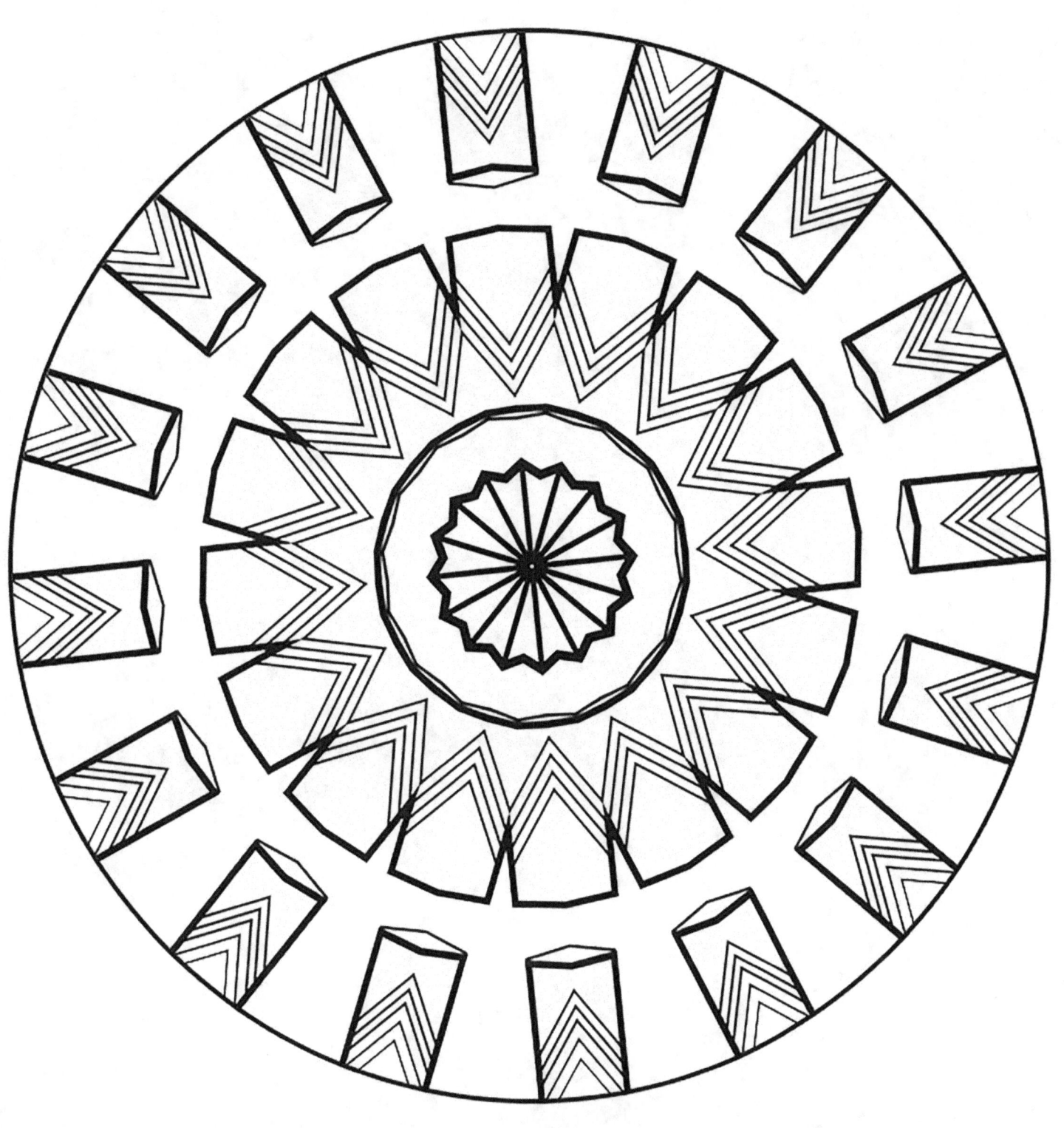

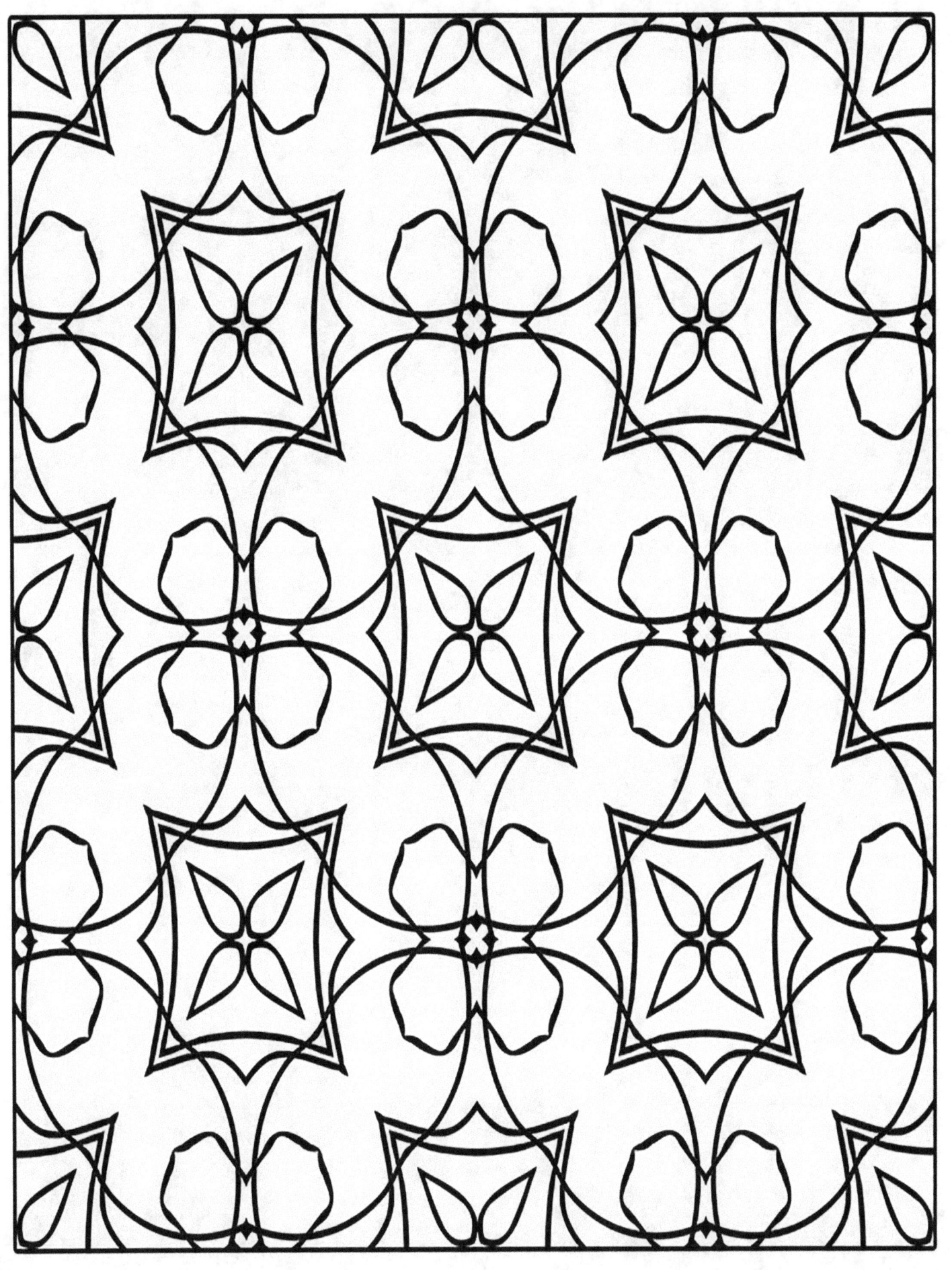

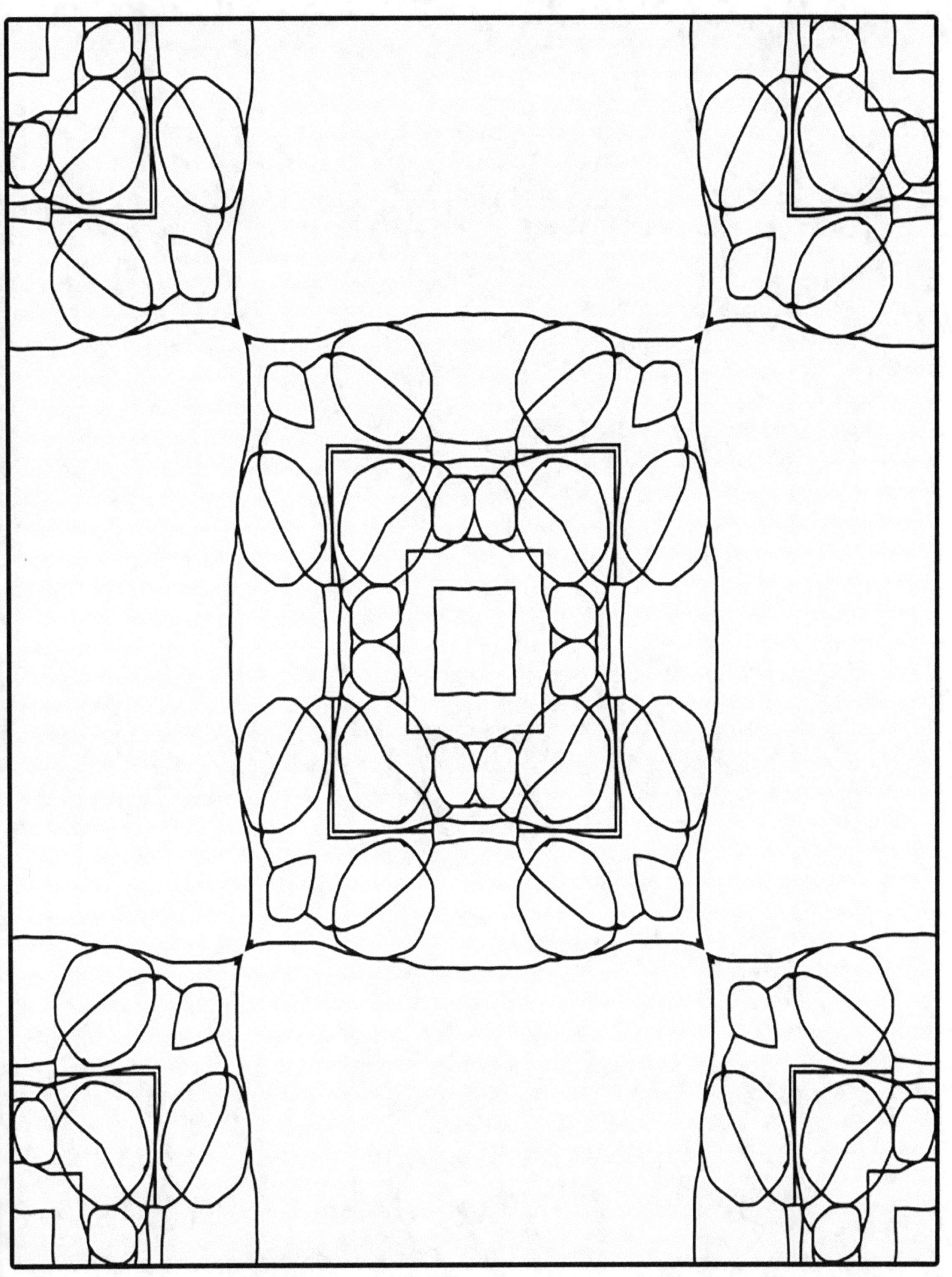

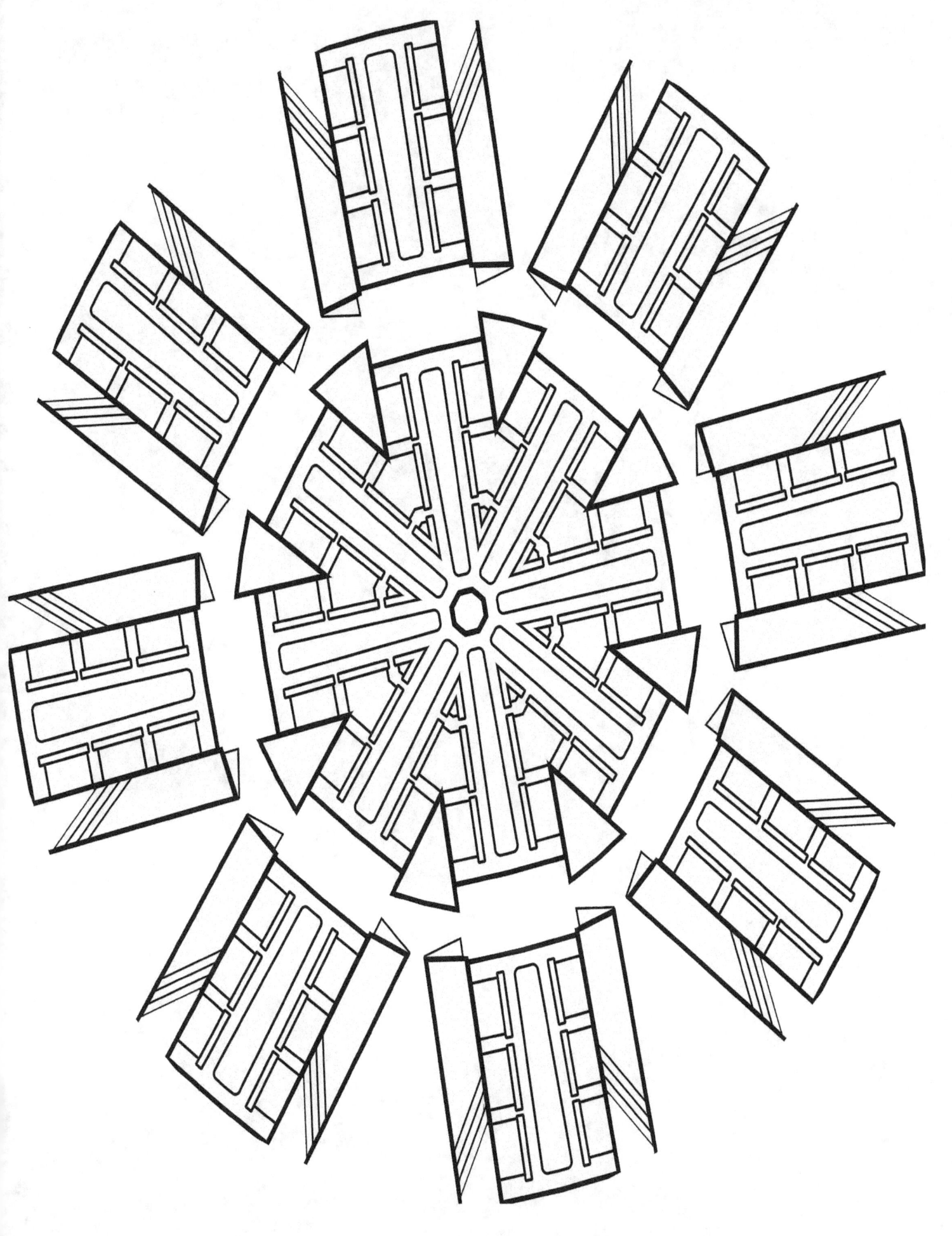

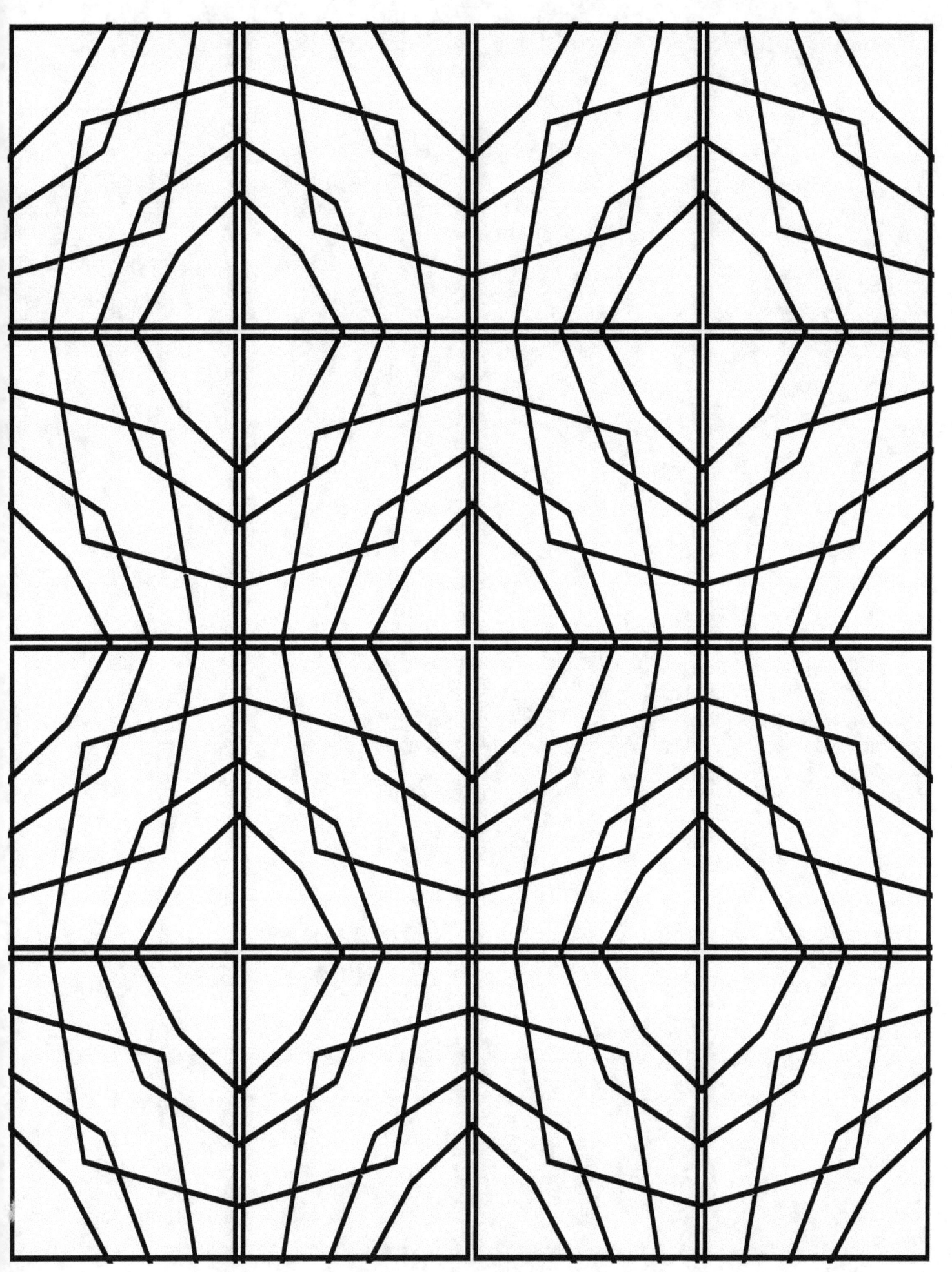

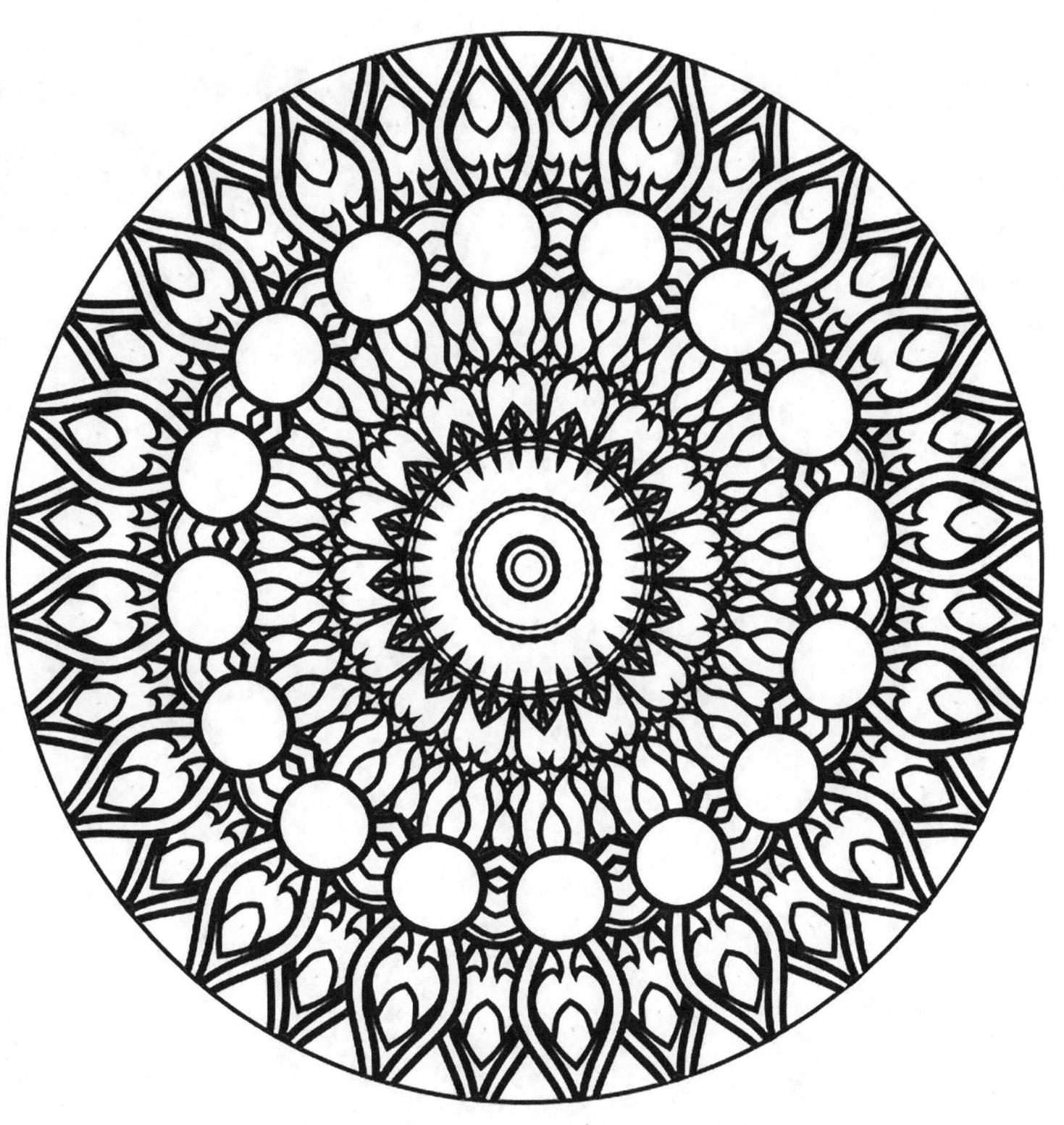

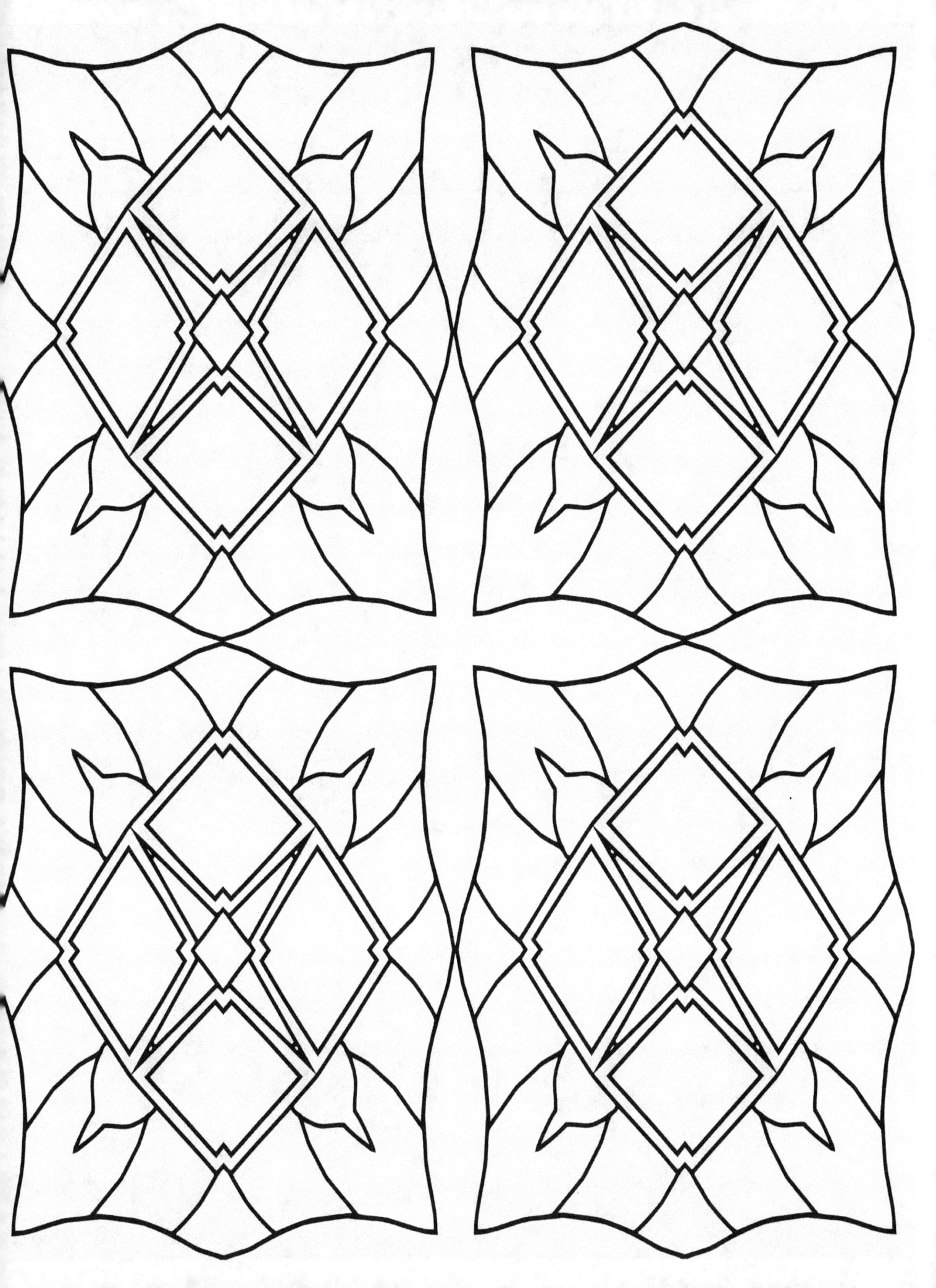

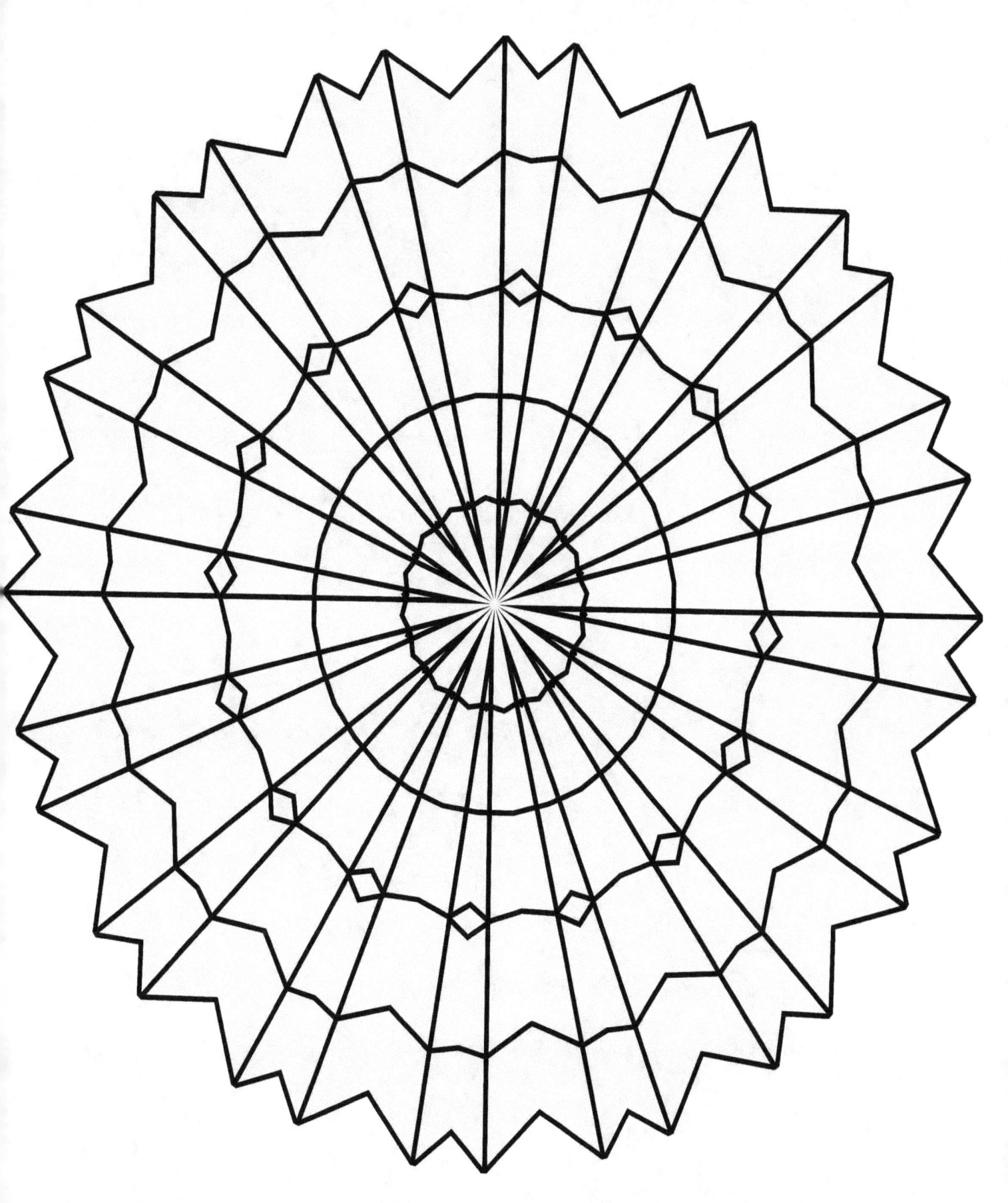

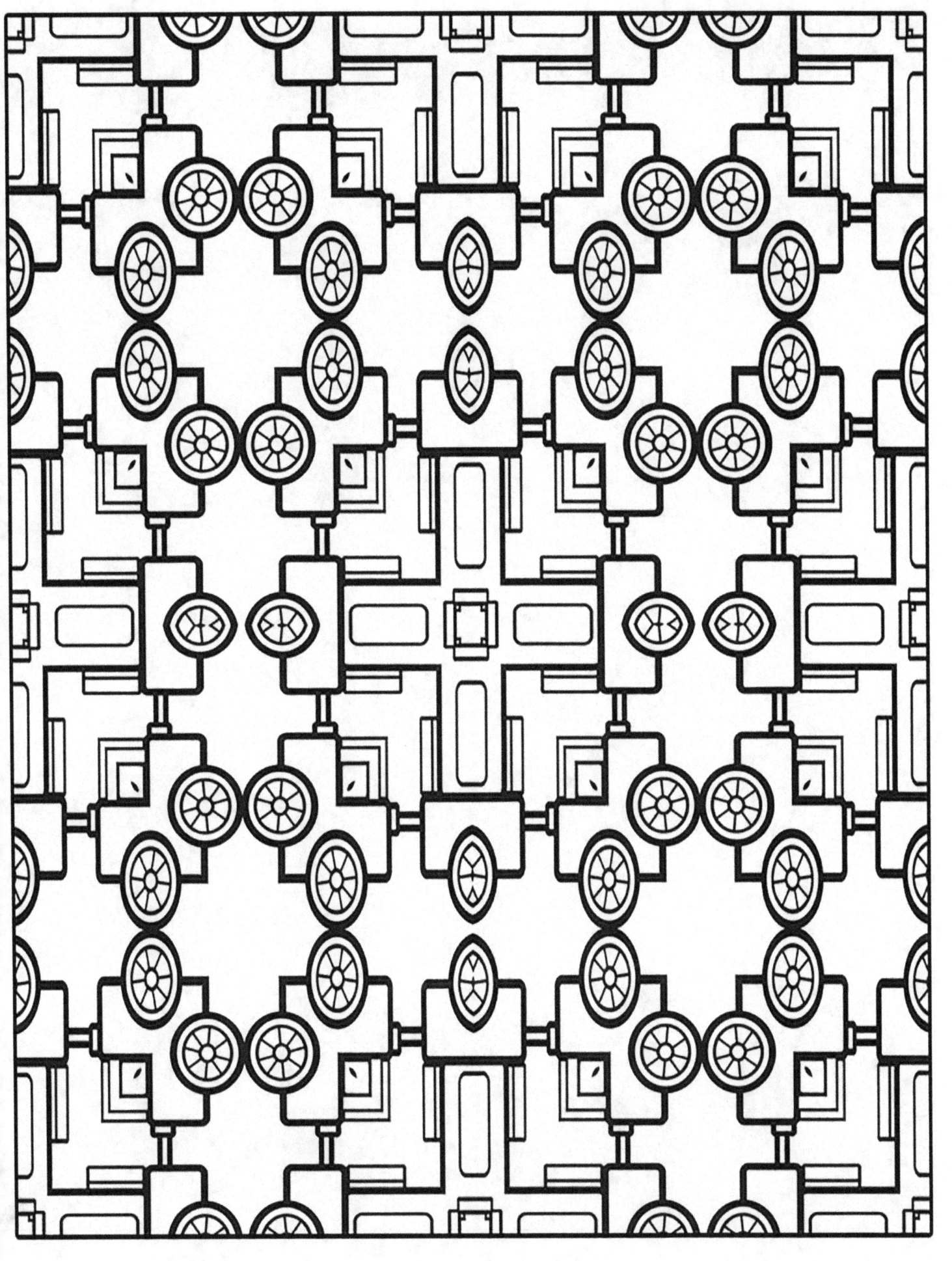

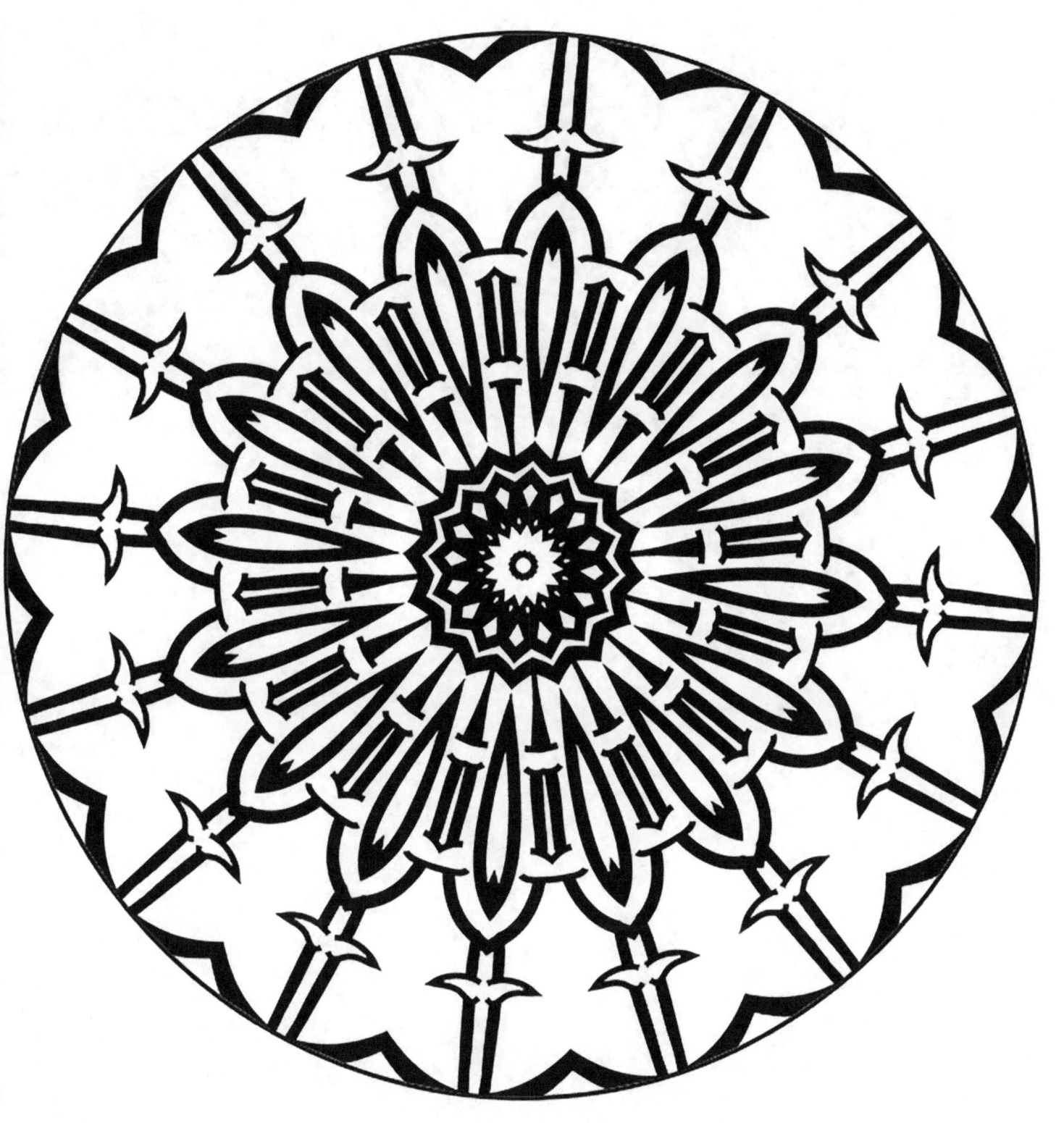

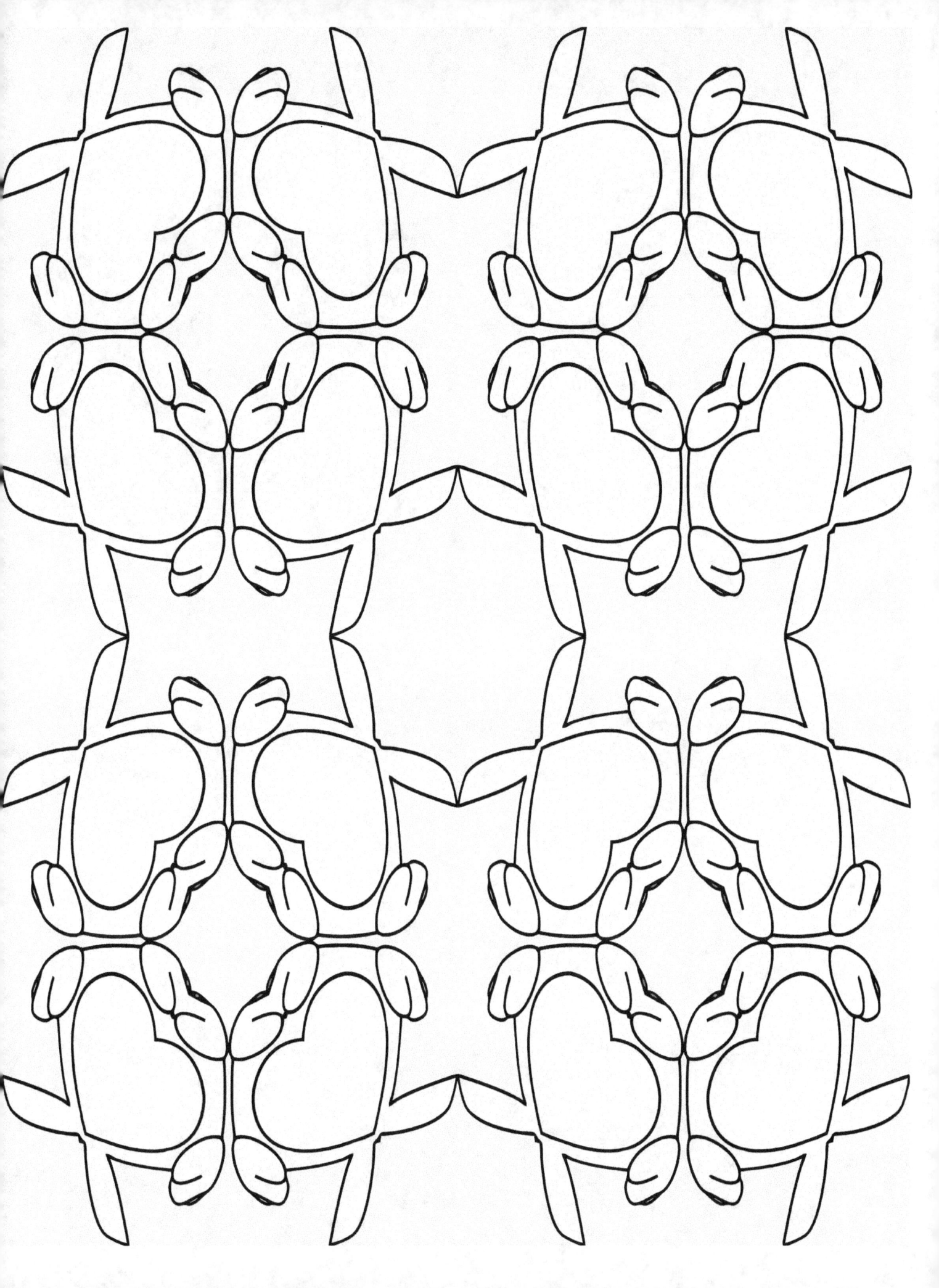

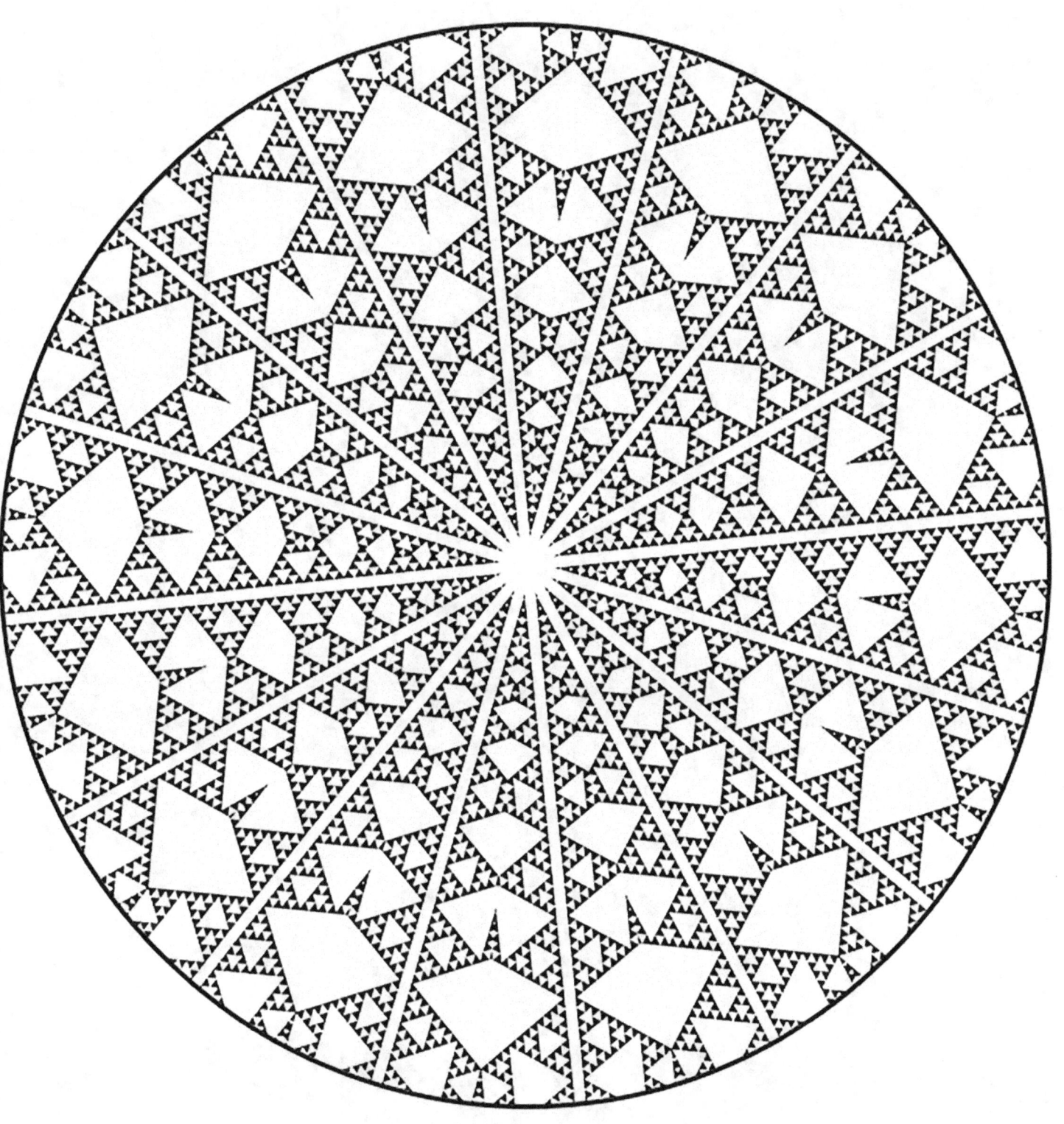

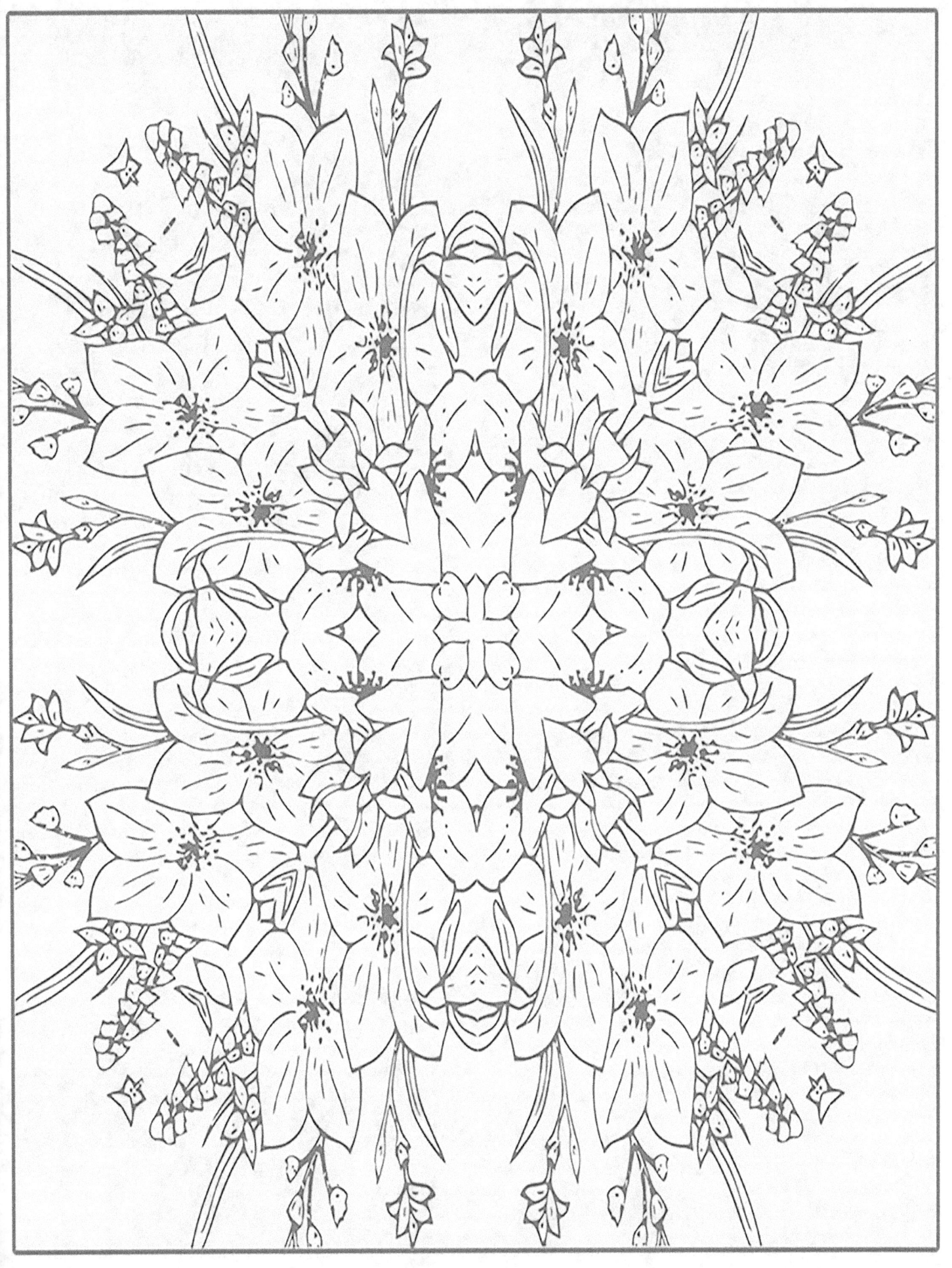

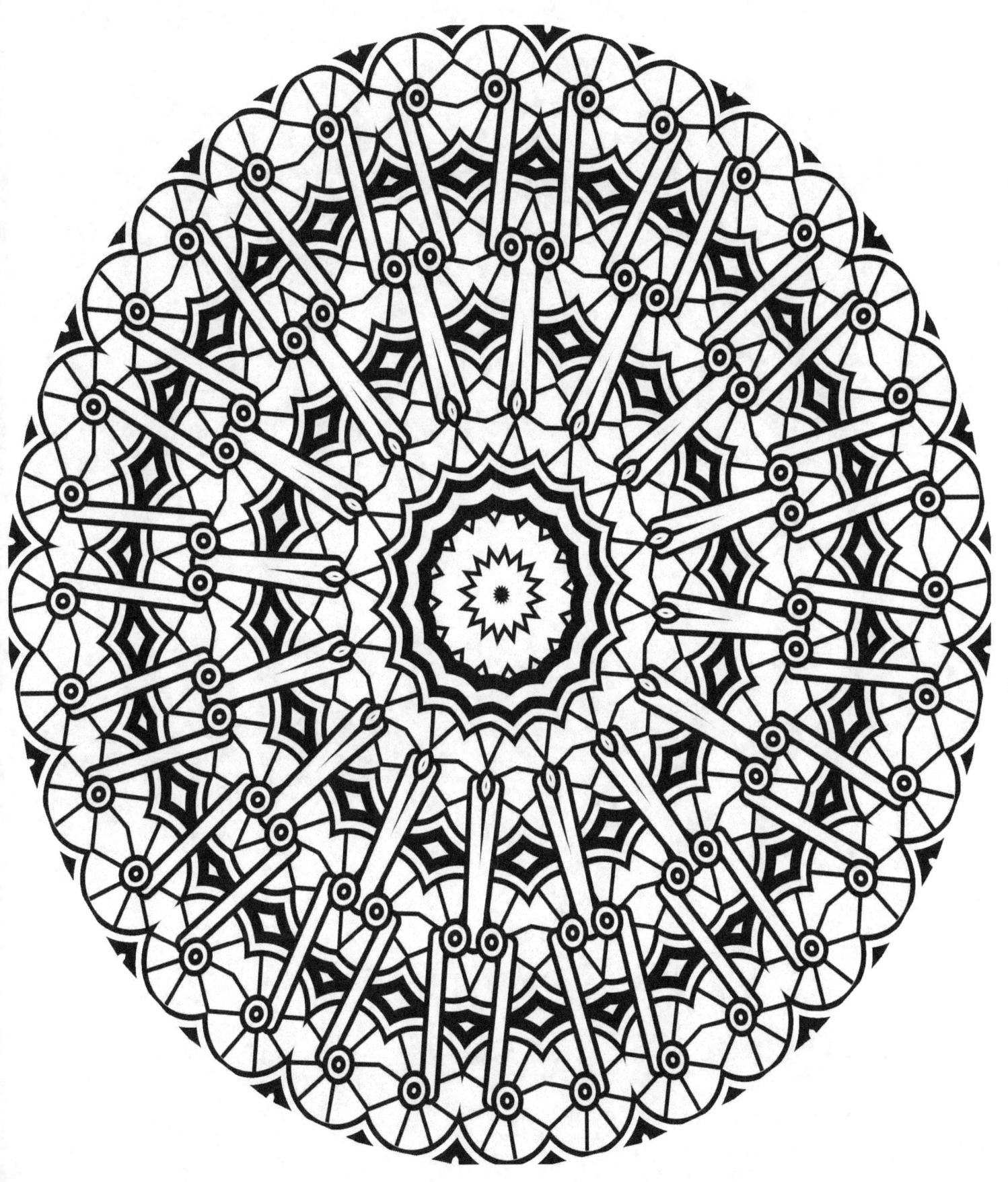

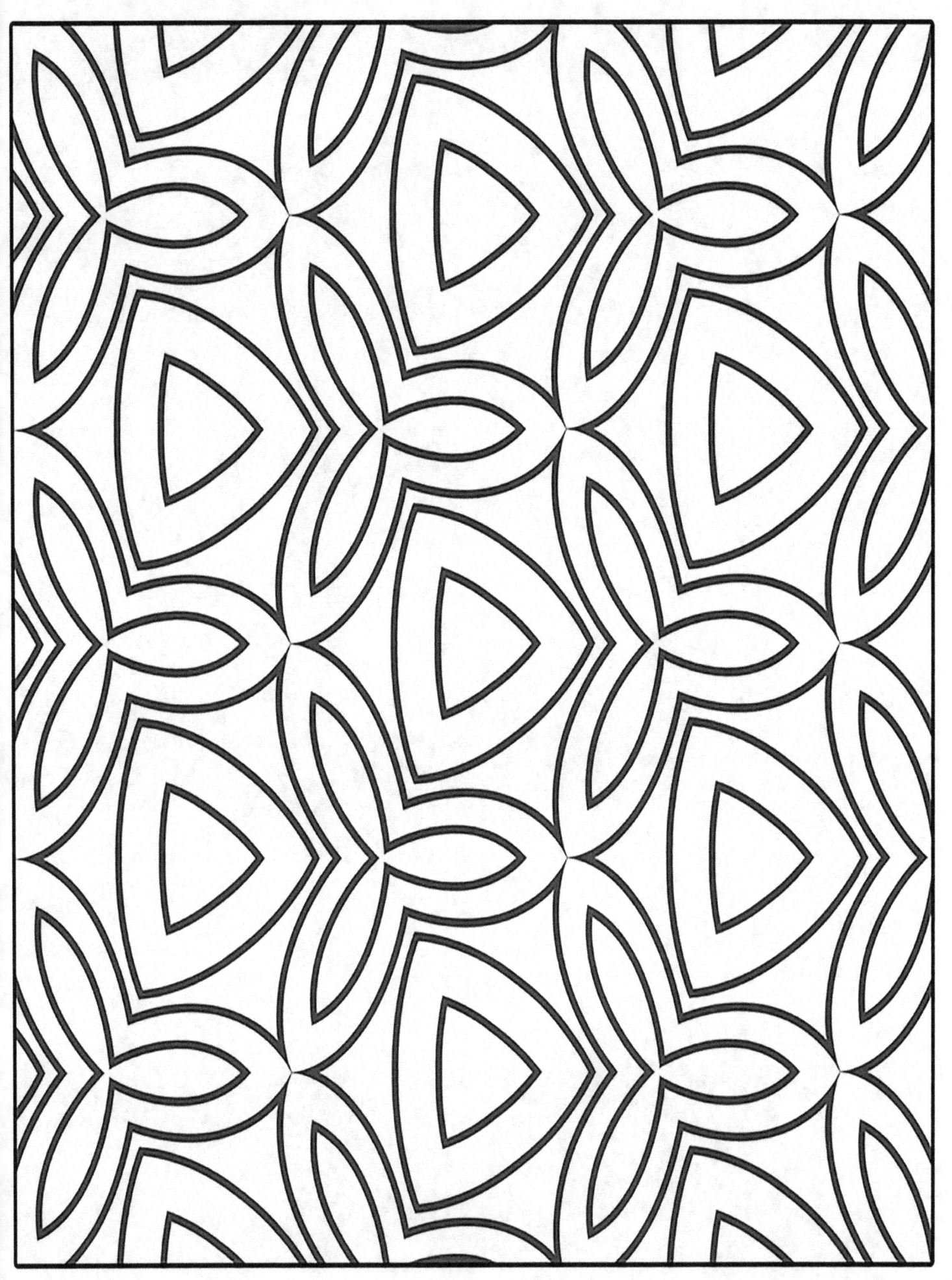

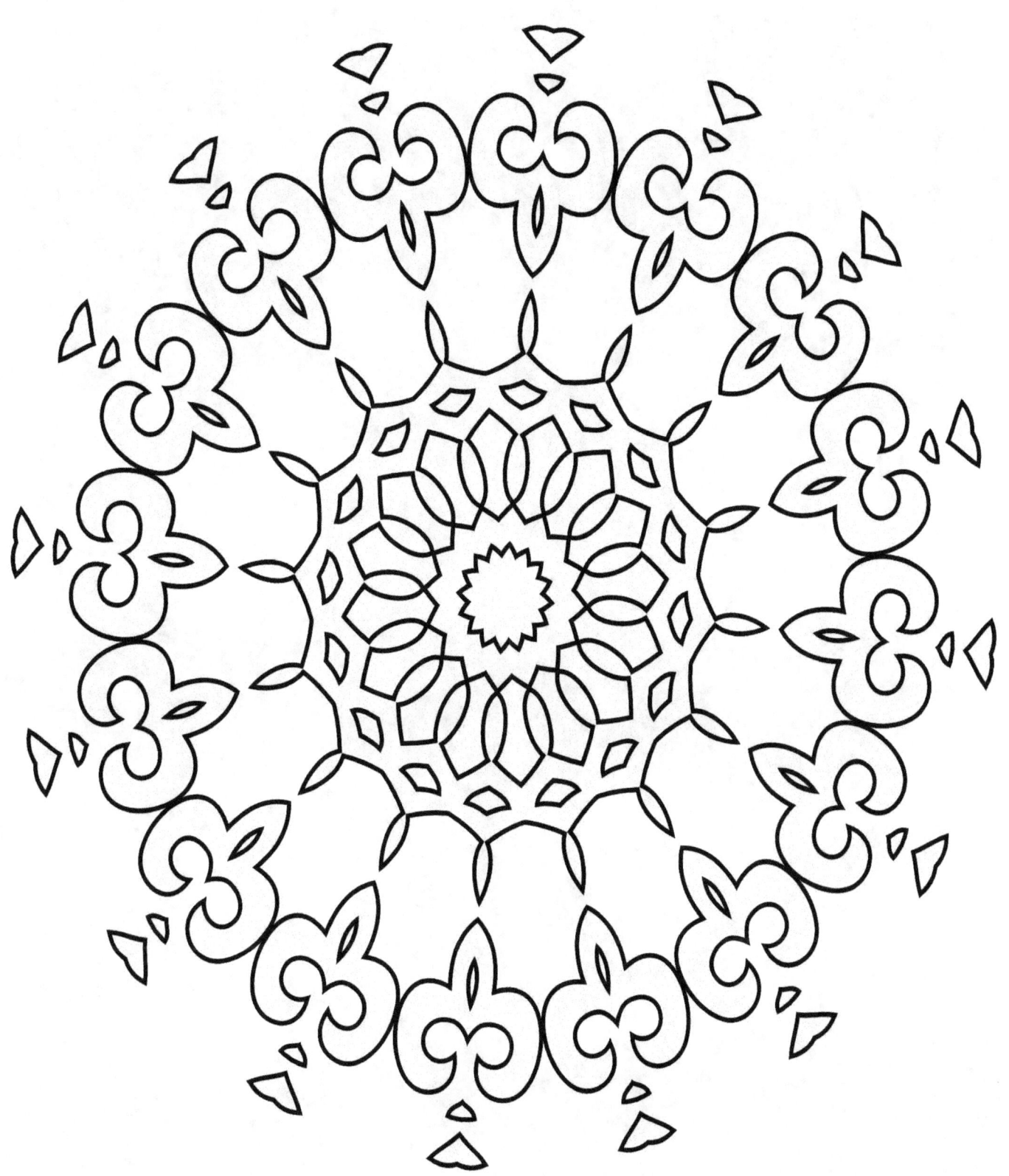

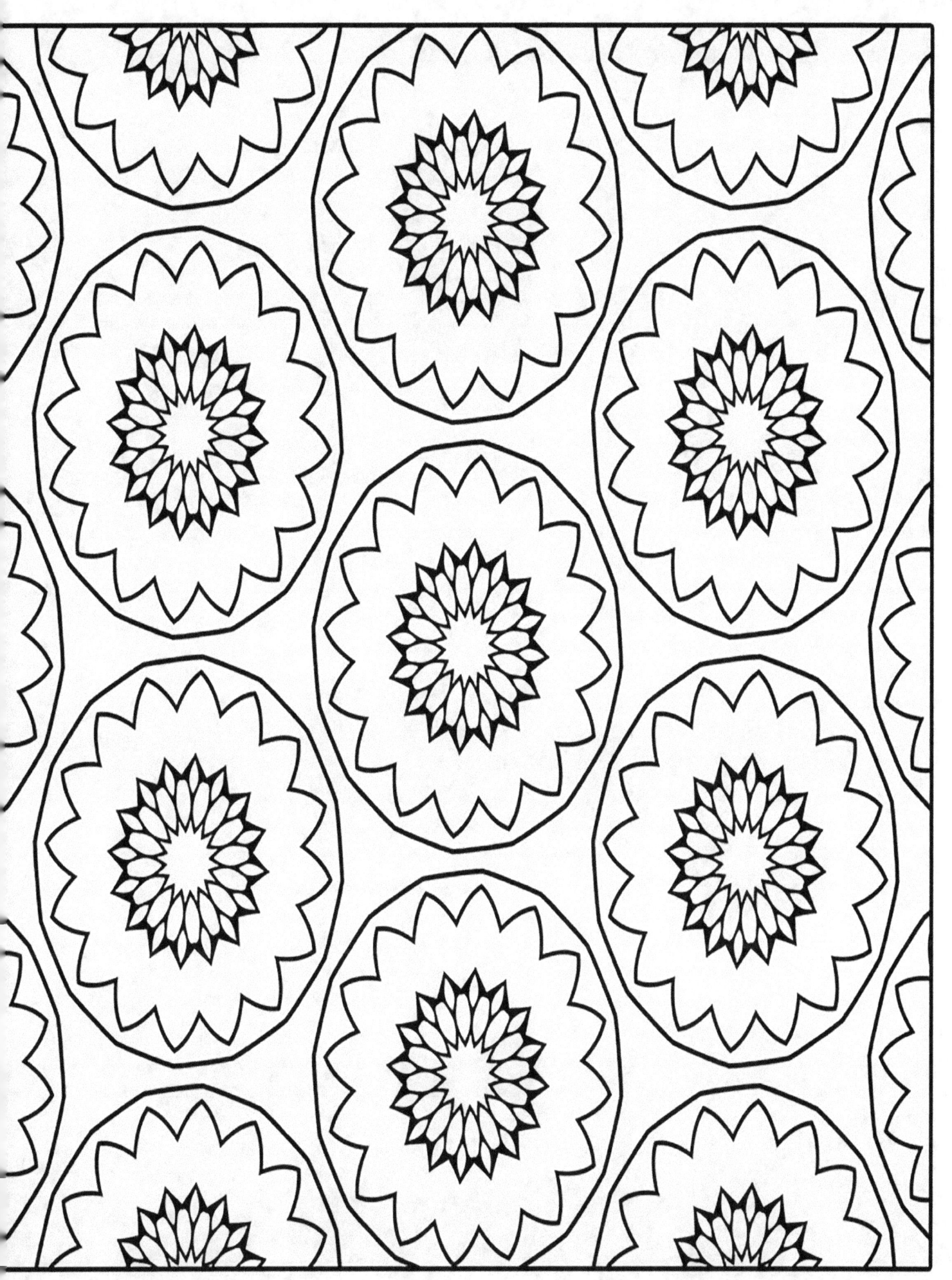

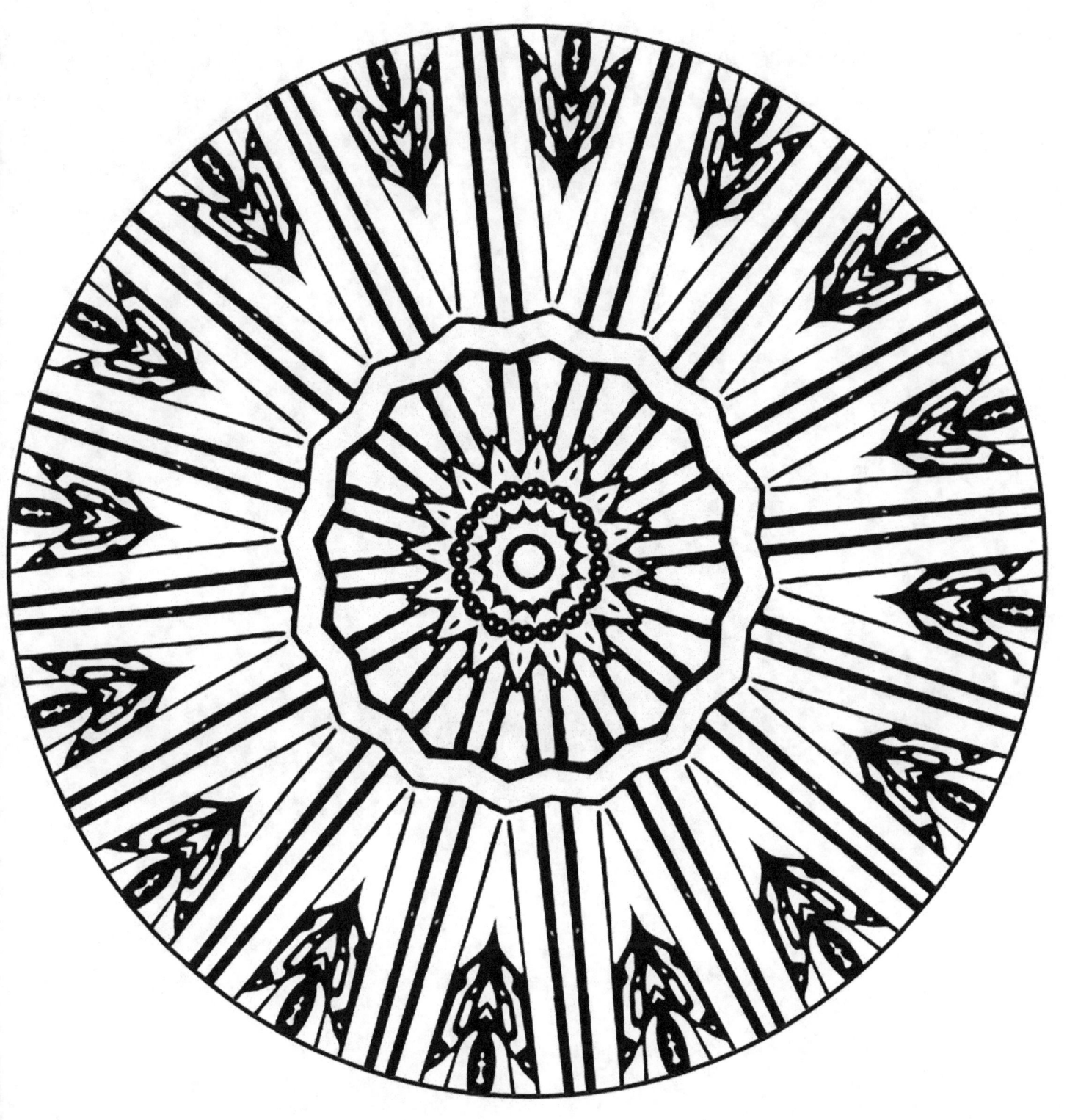

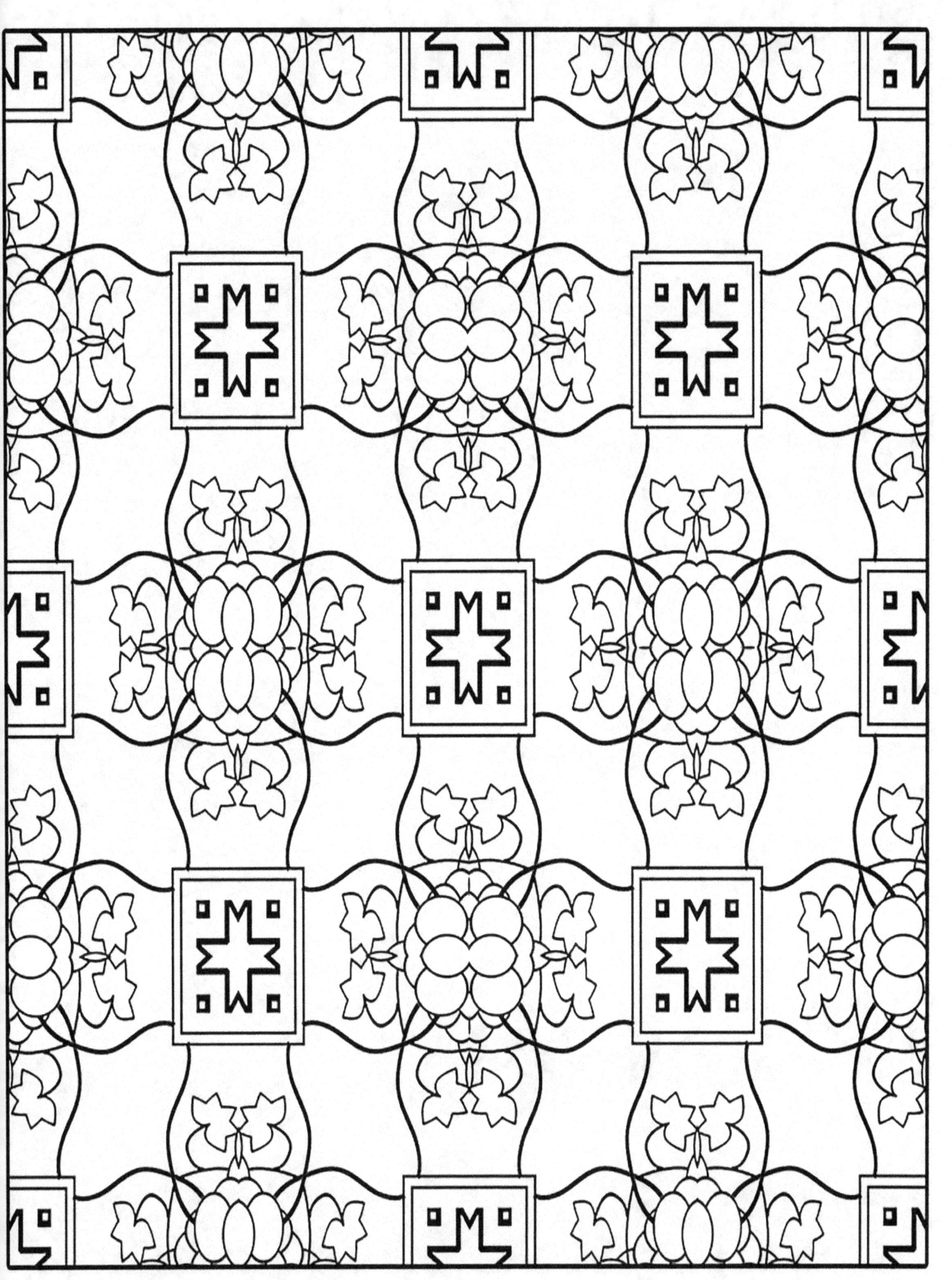

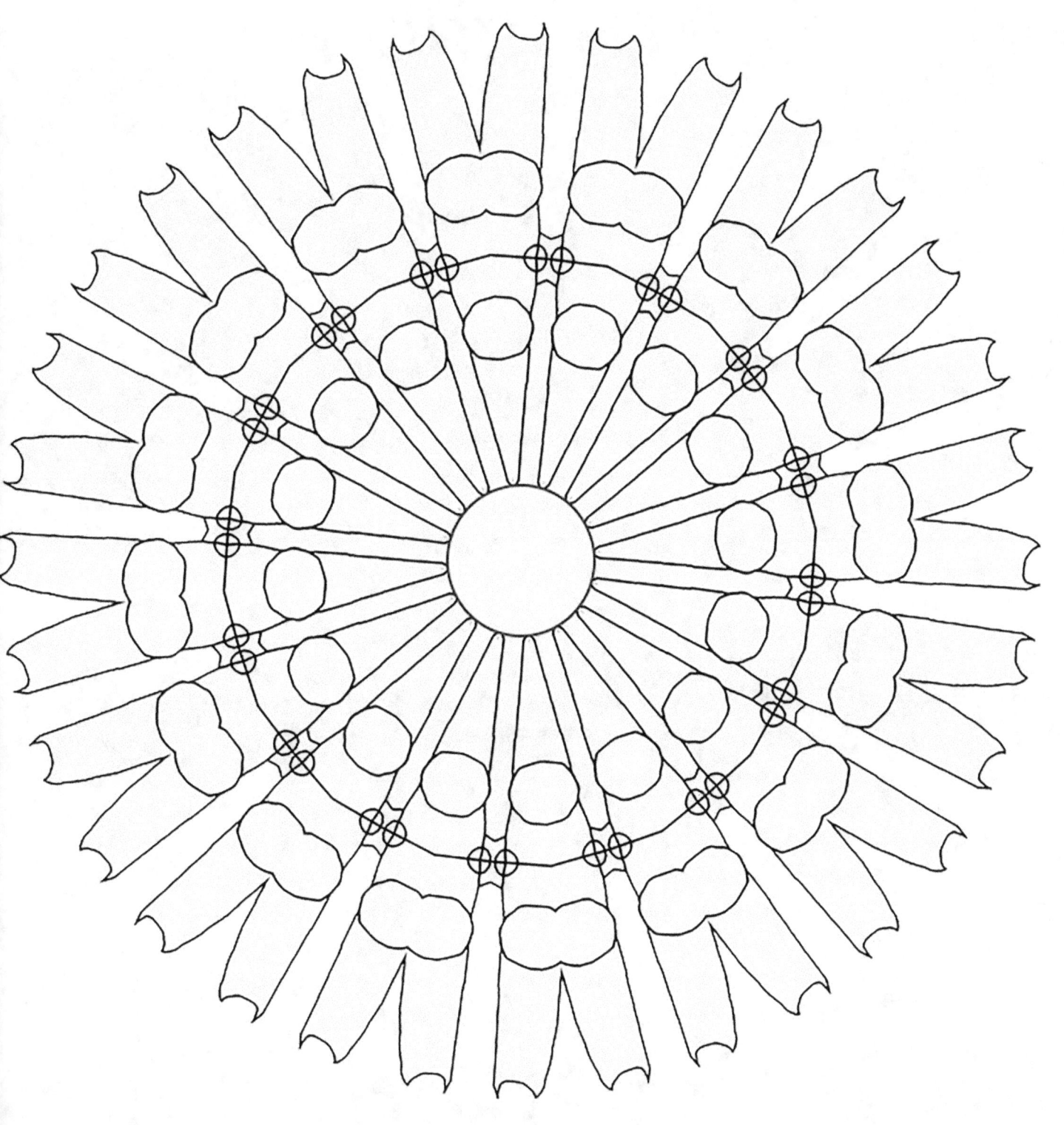

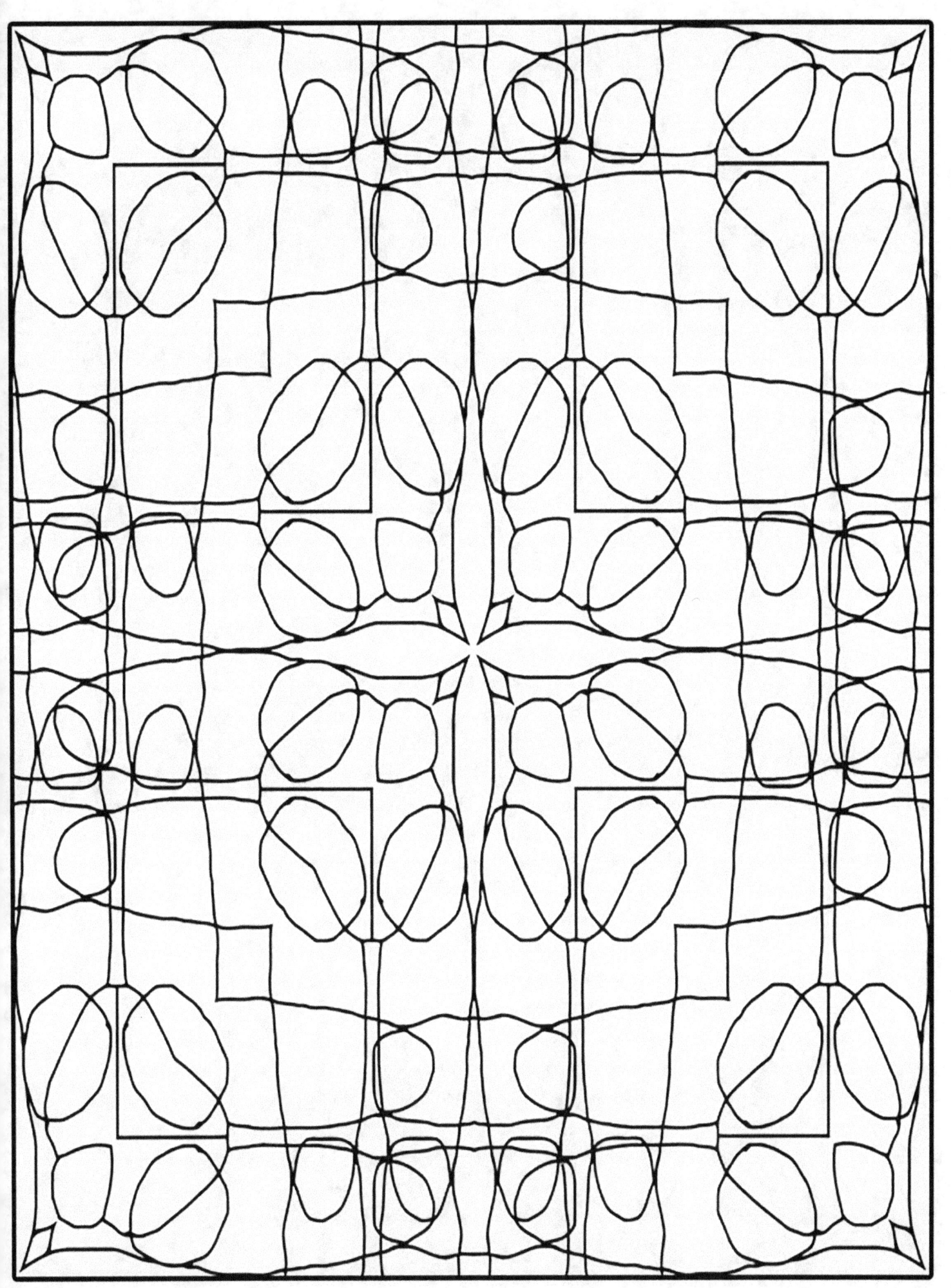

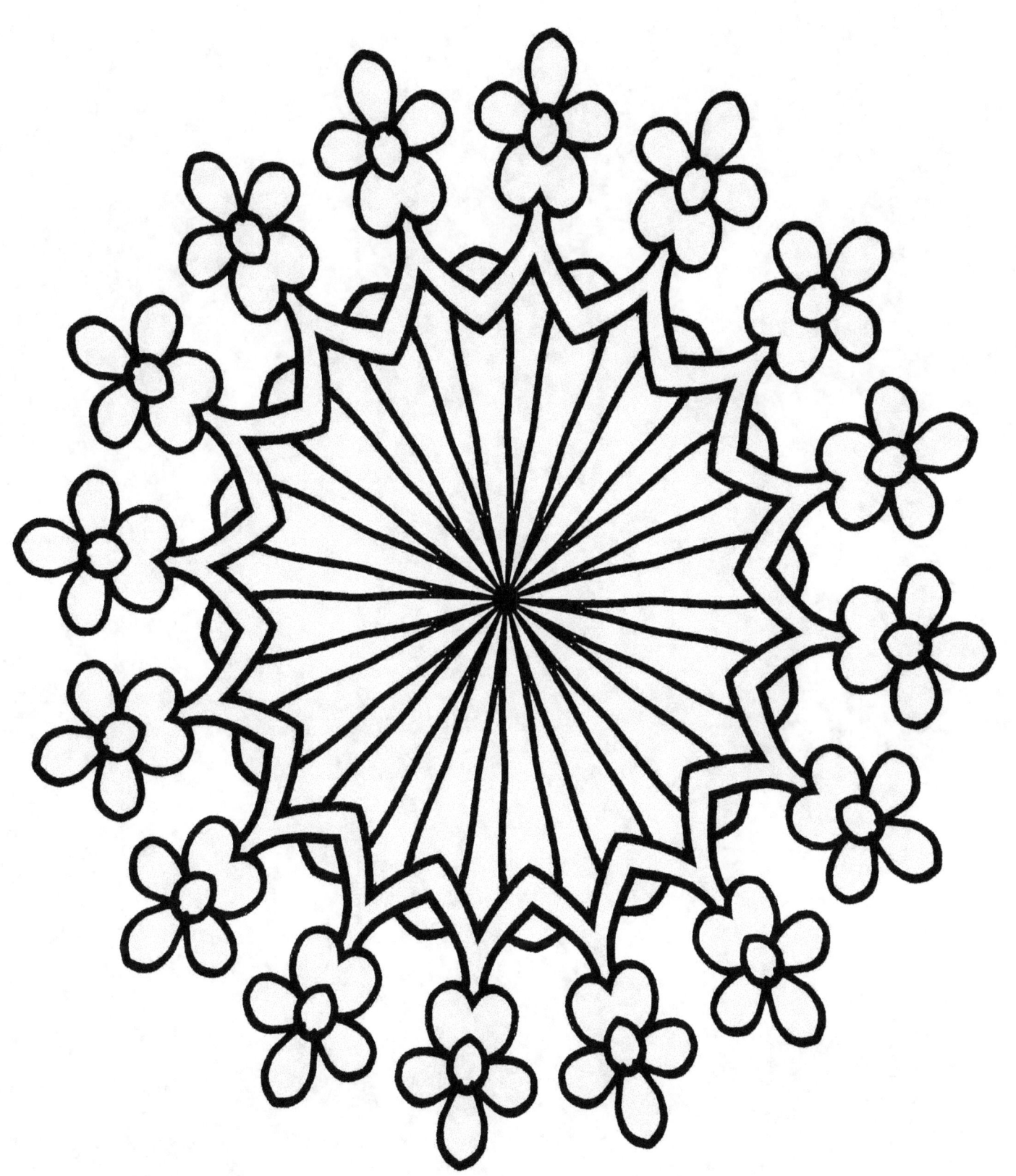

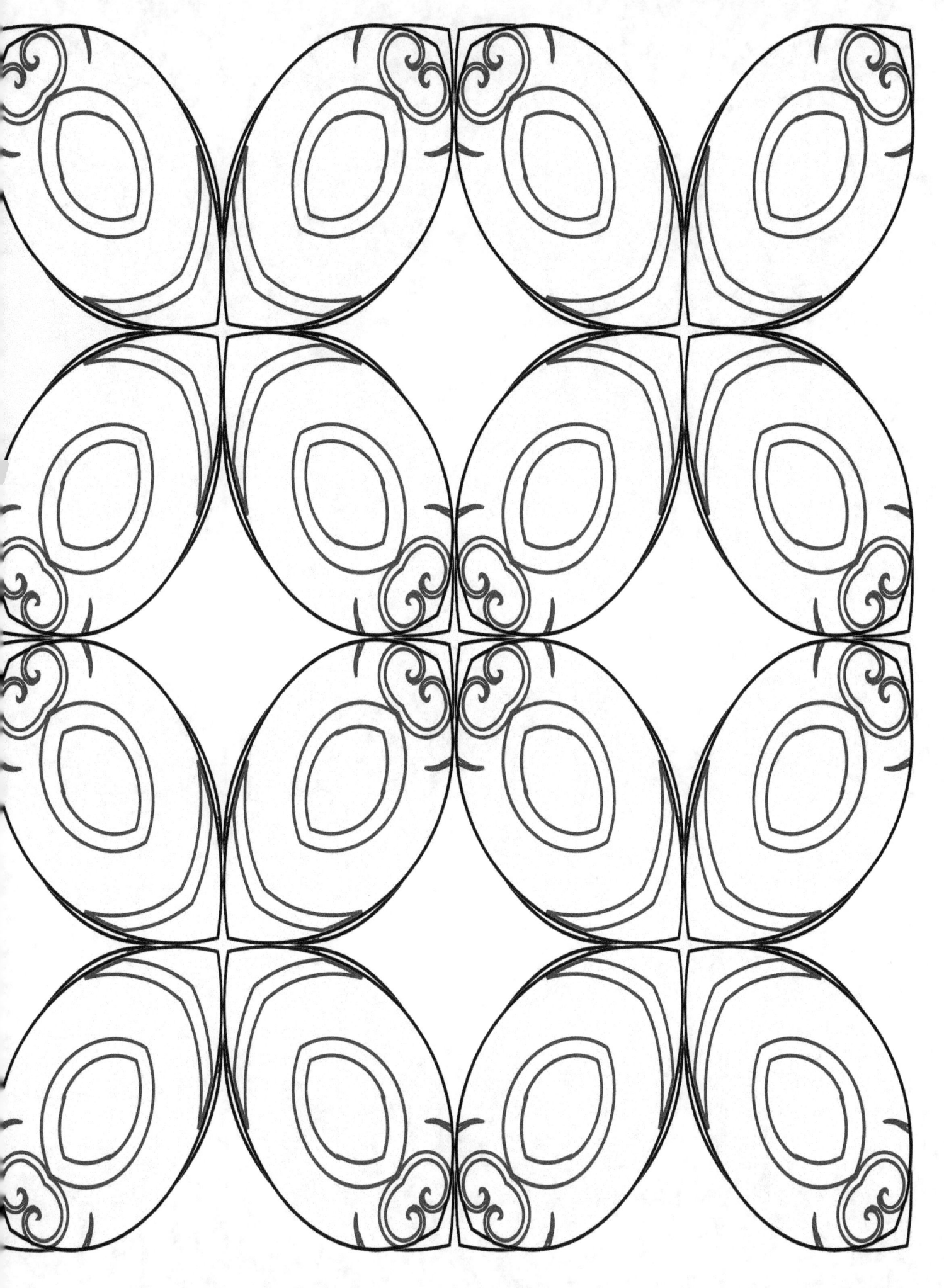

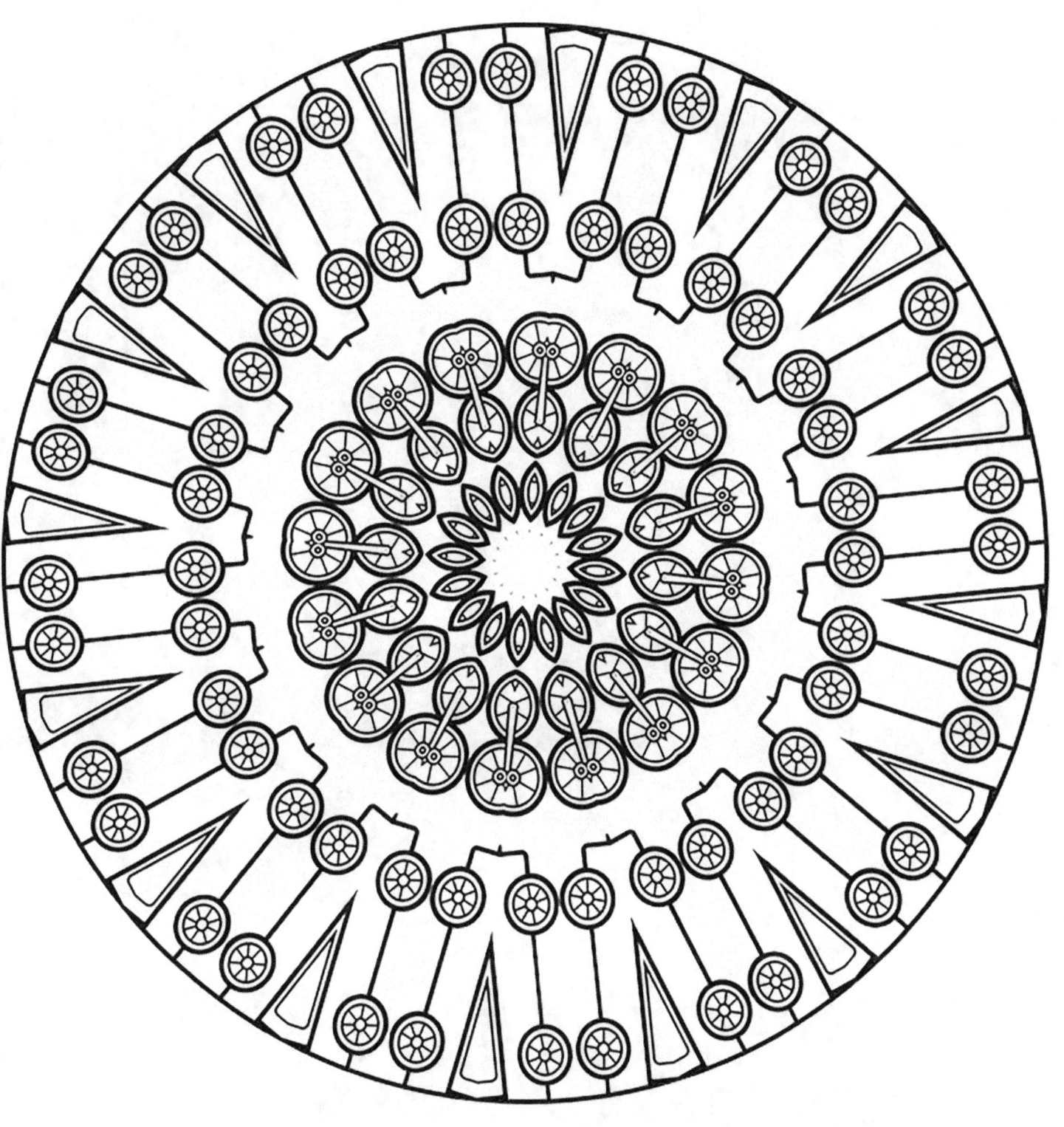

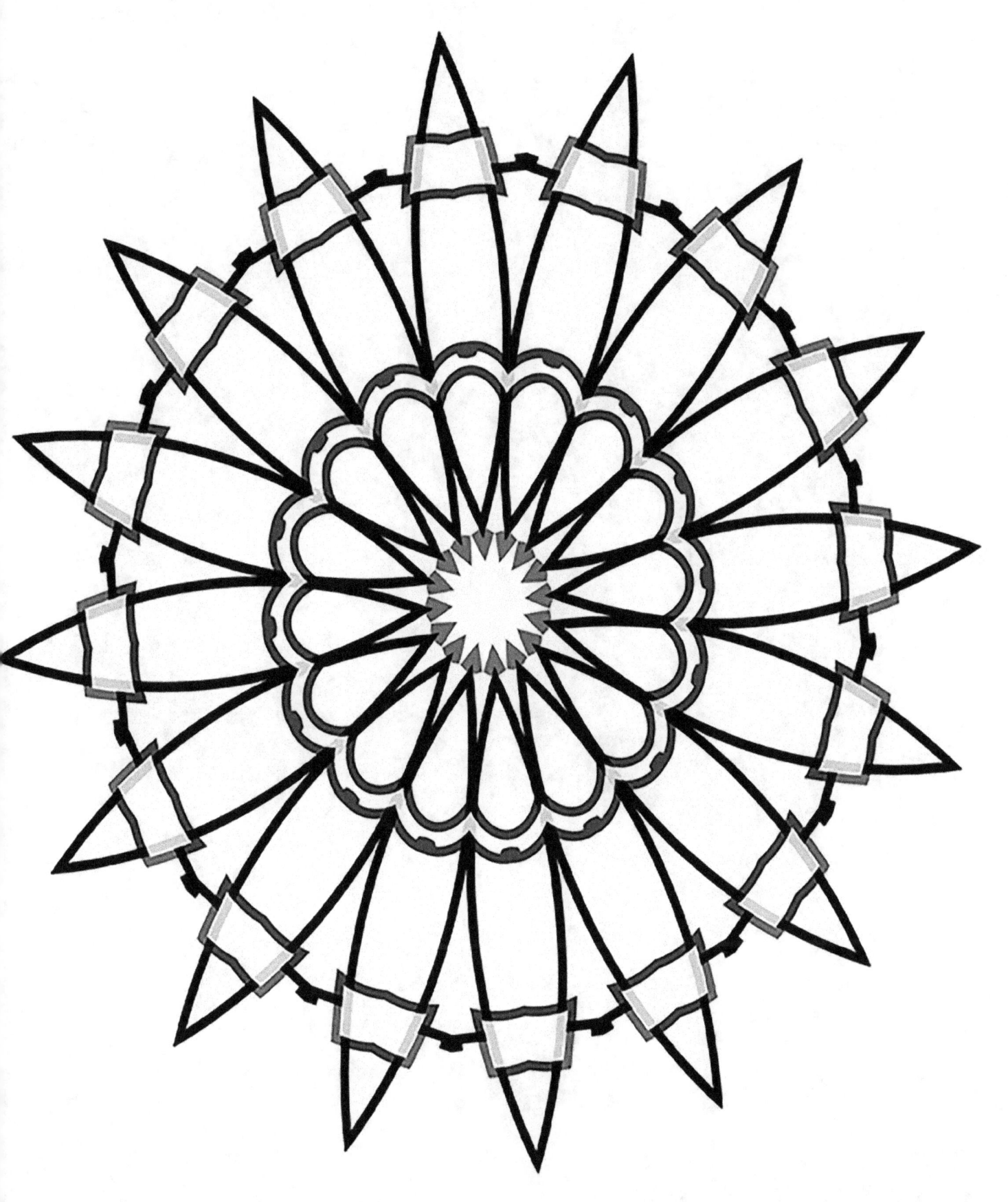

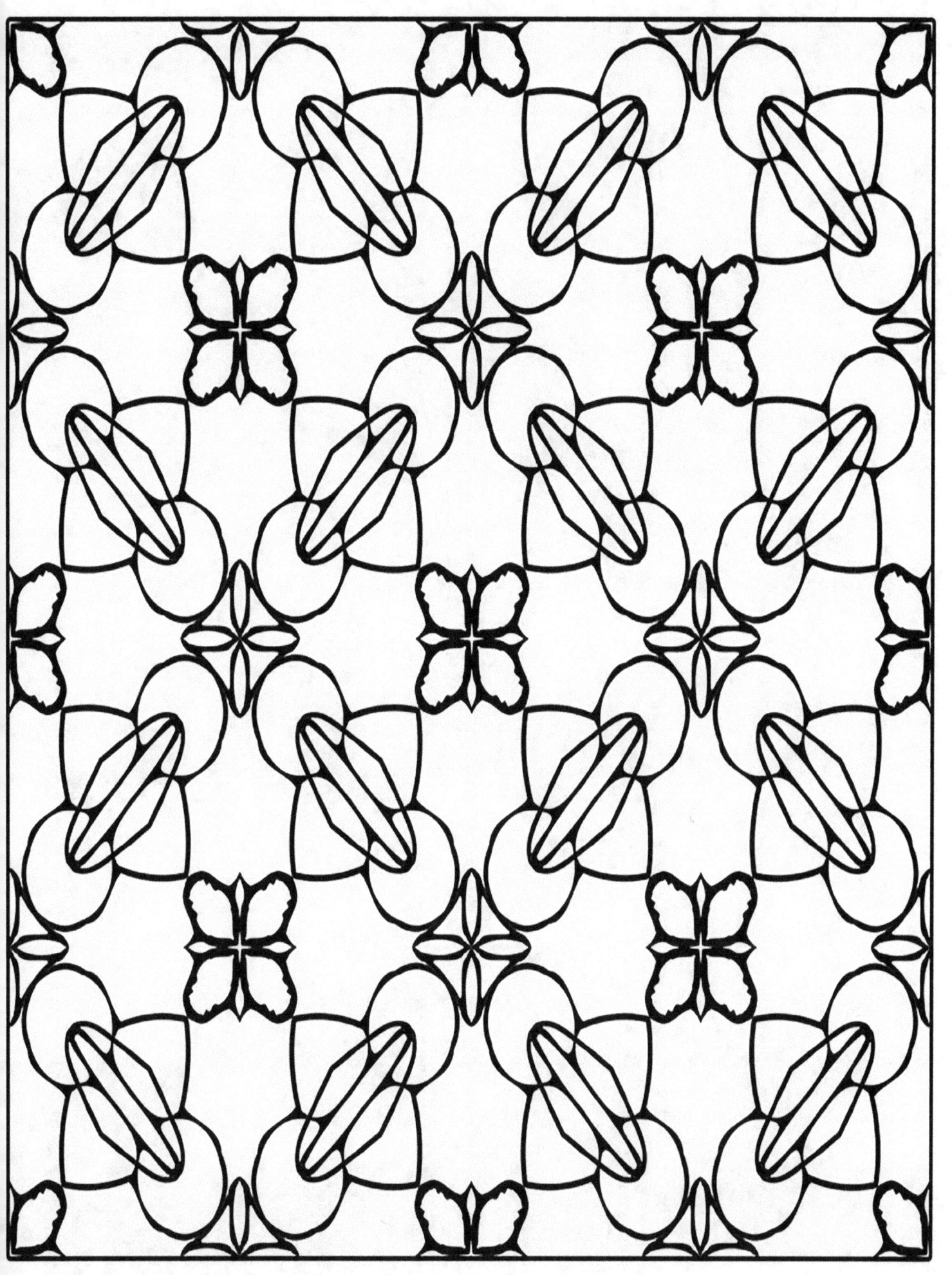

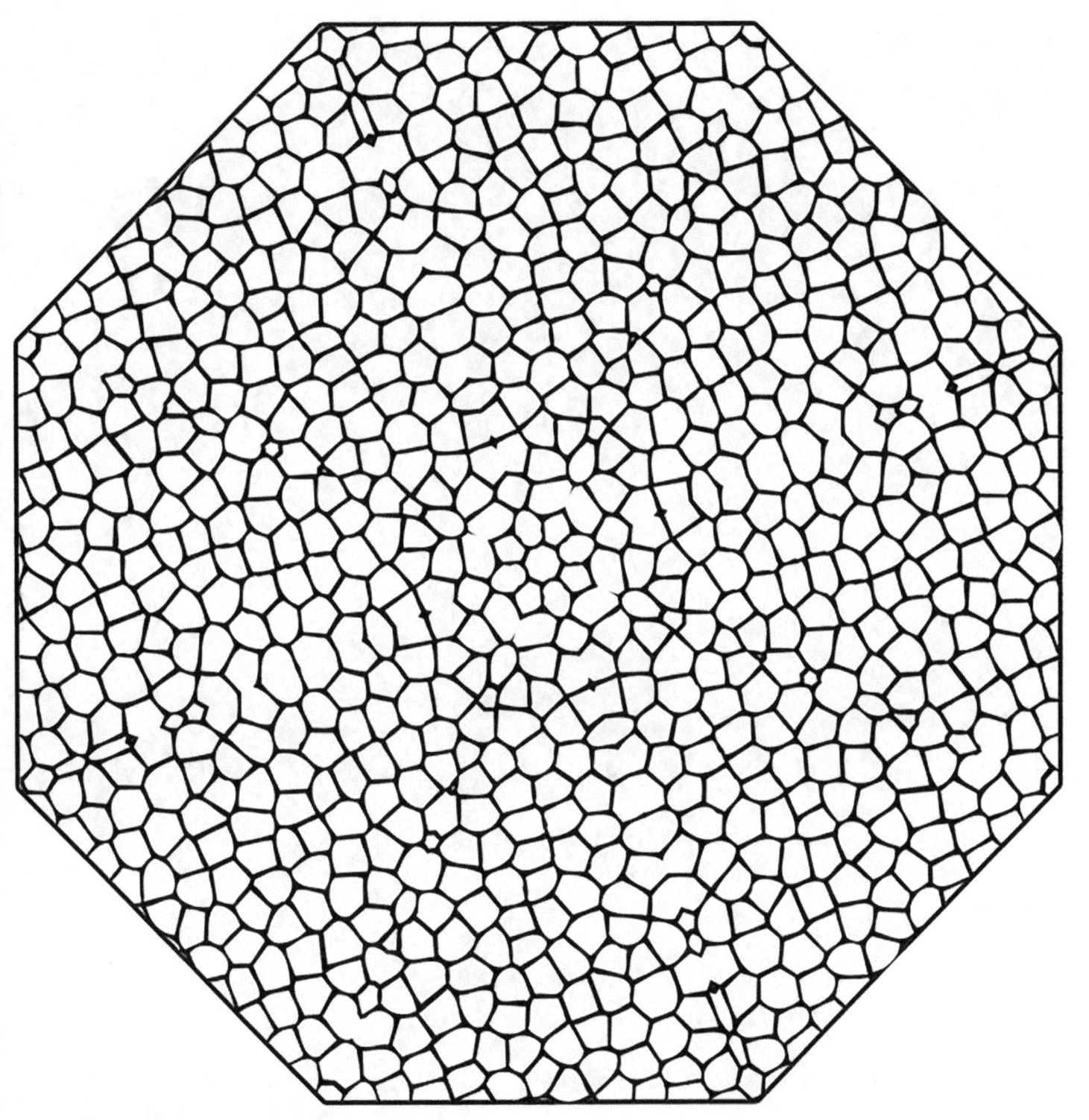

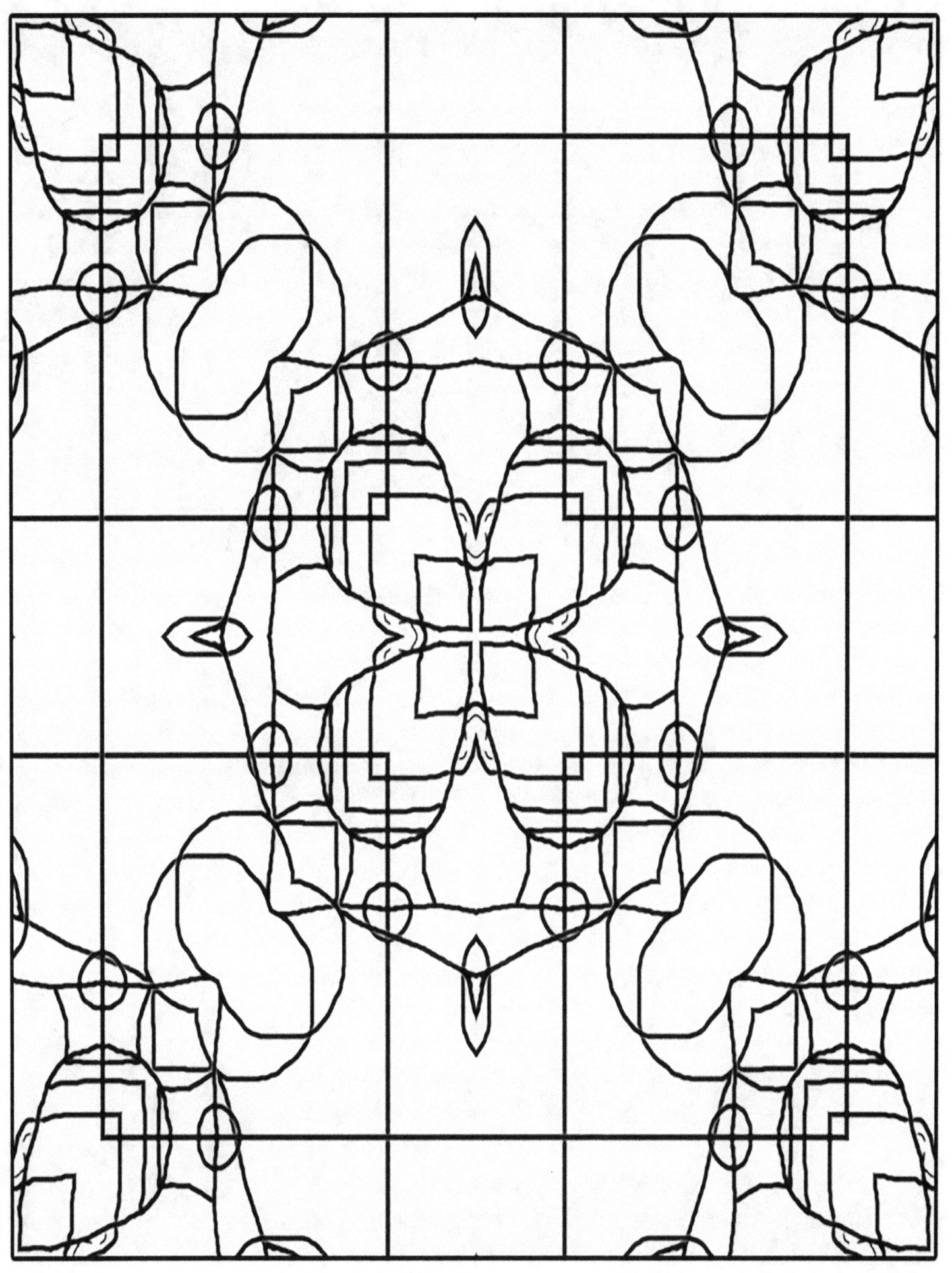

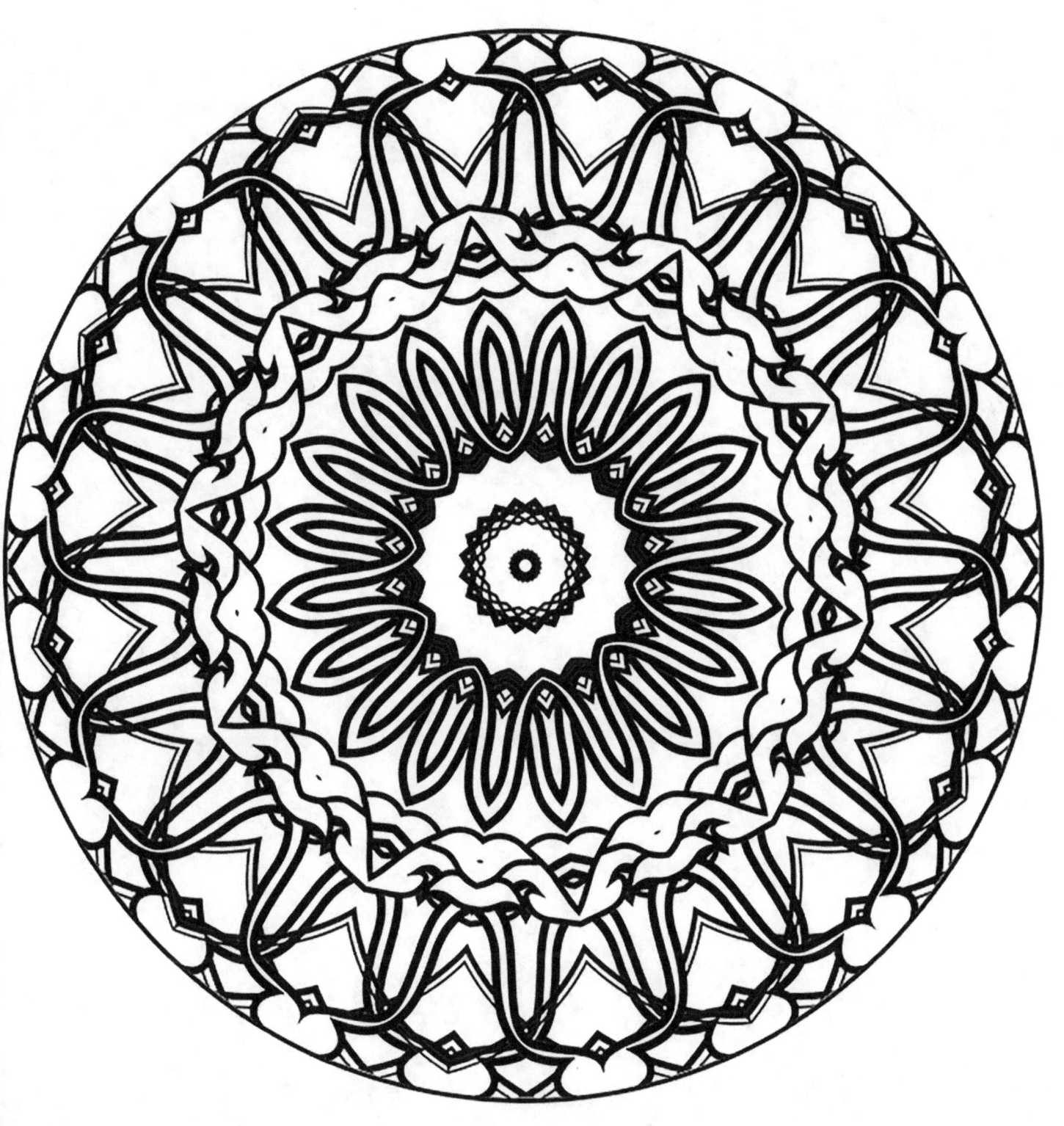

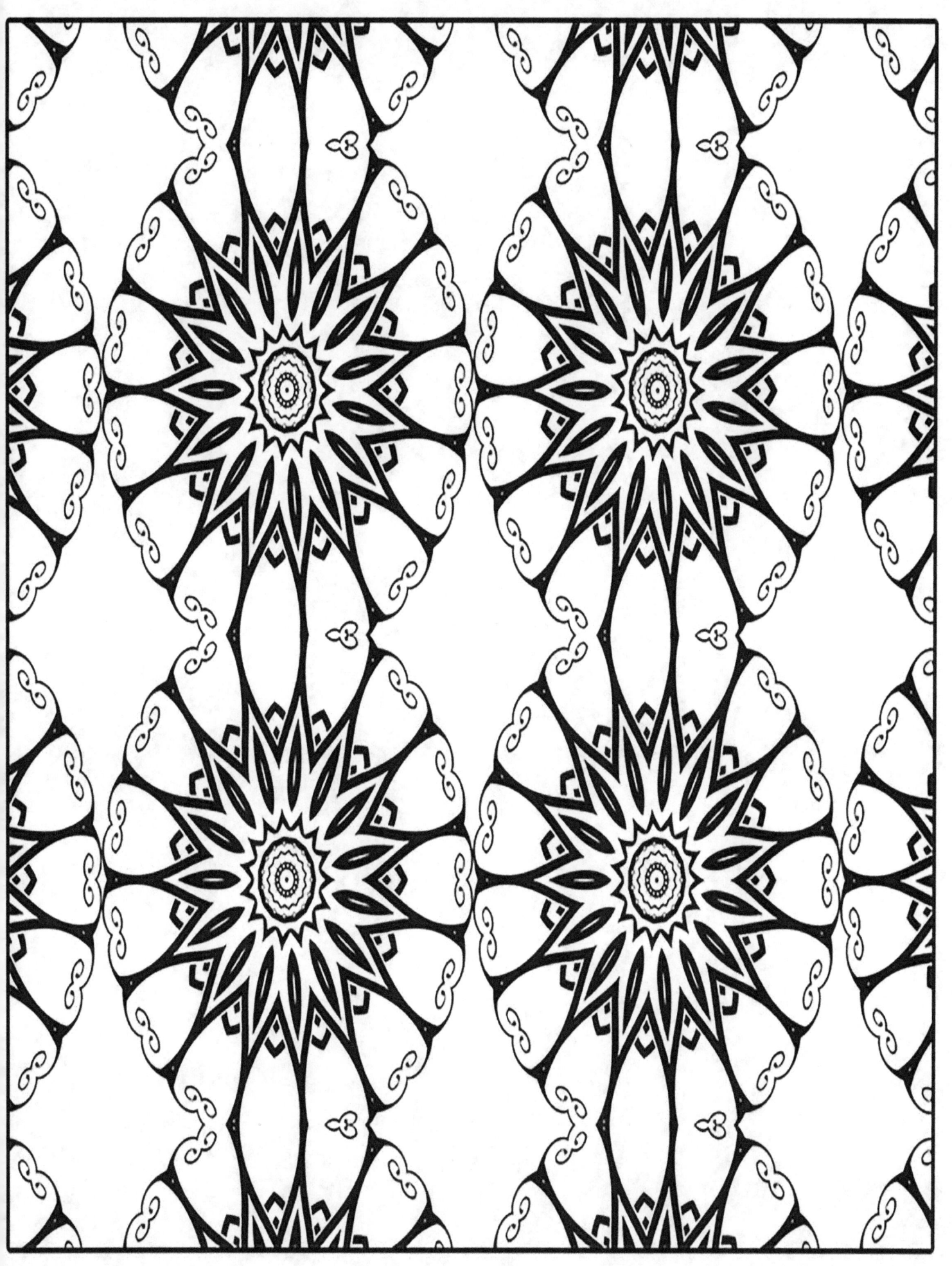

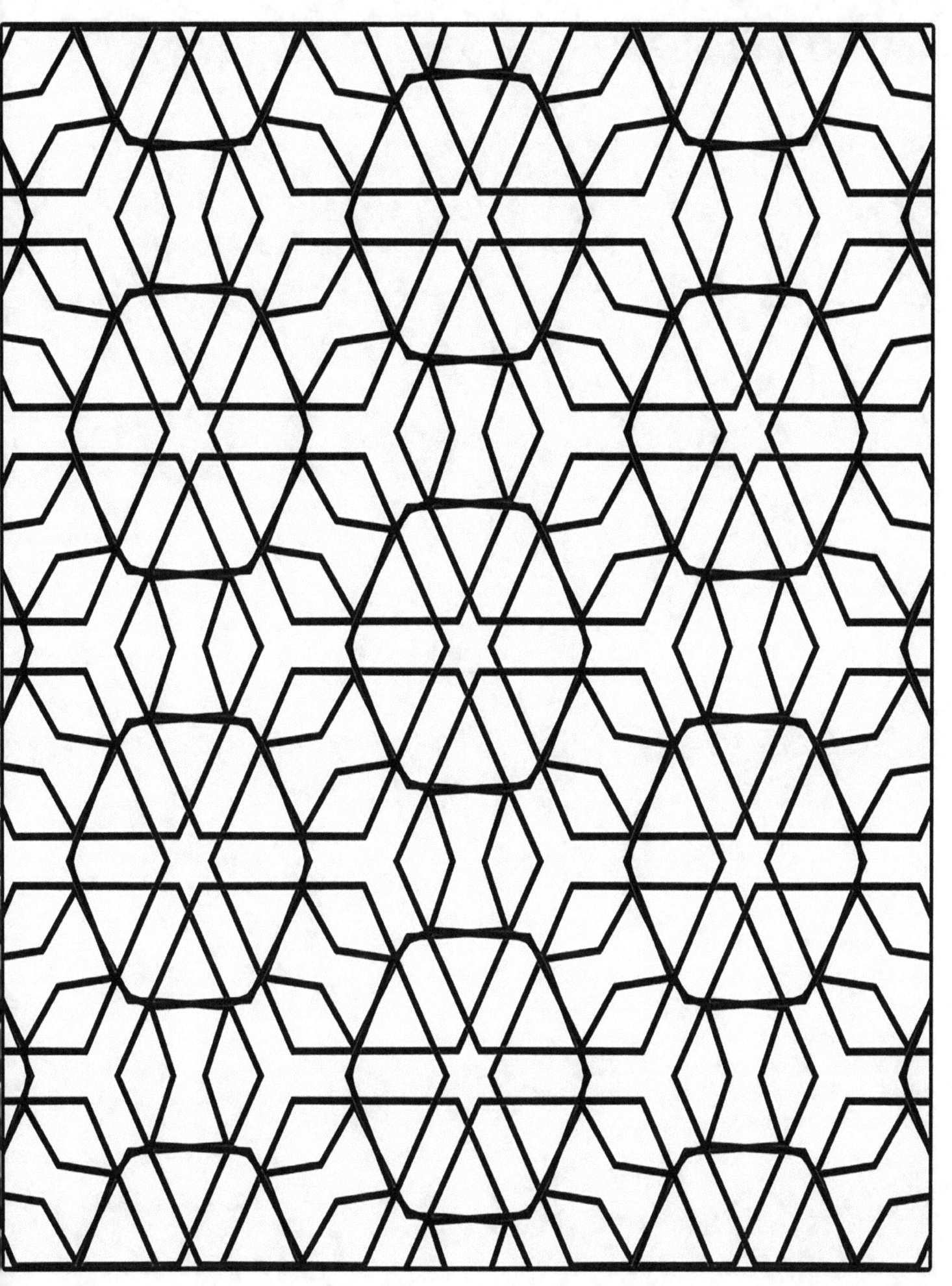

Be Happy Coloring Books

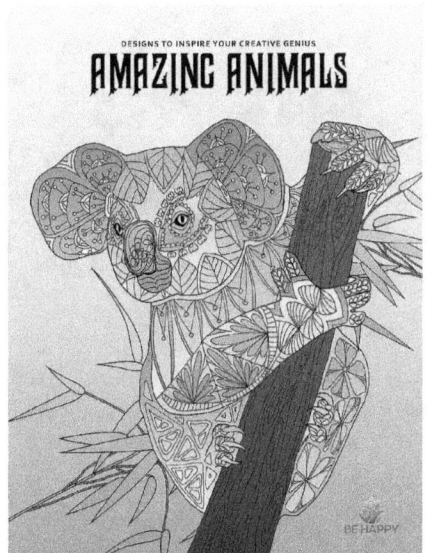

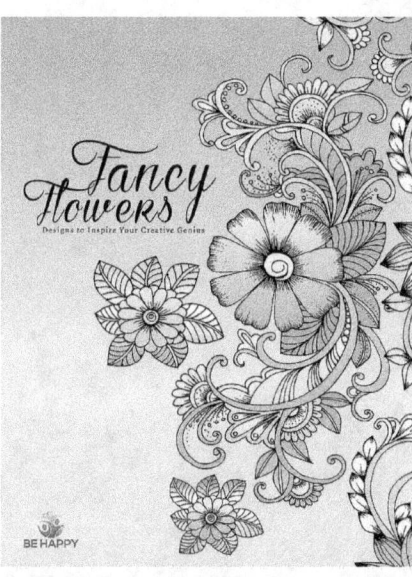

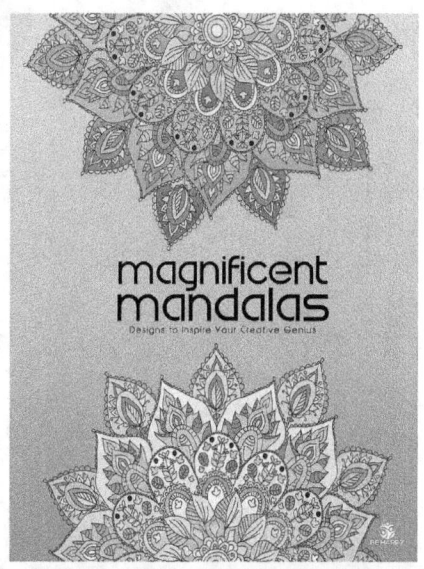

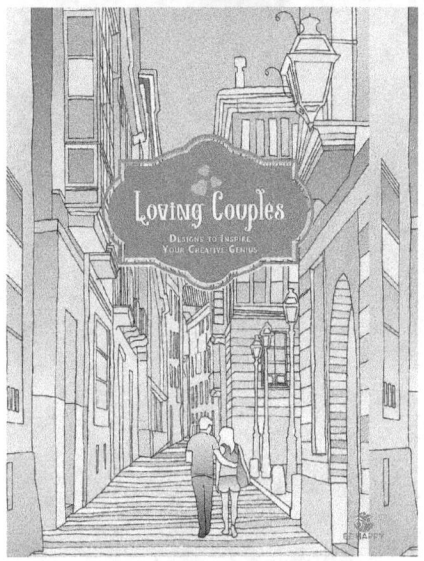

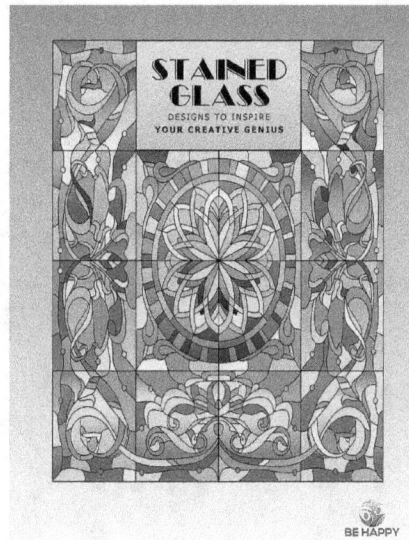

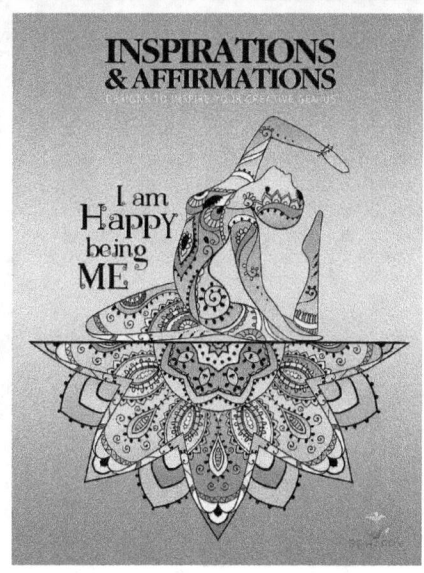

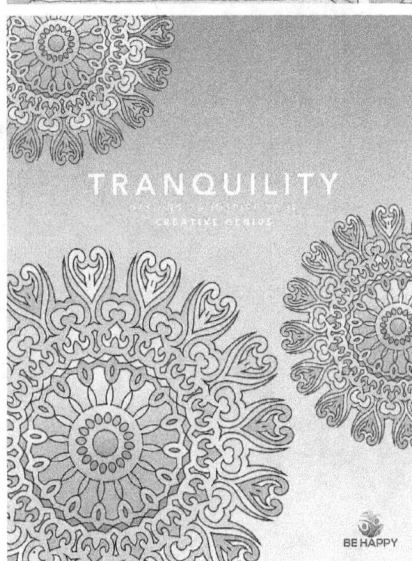

Stay tuned, more coloring books to come.
Our artists are passionately creating
new coloring pages to help inspire
your creative genius.

www.BeHappyColoringBooks.com

www.ingramcontent.com/pod-product-compliance
Lightning Source LLC
Chambersburg PA
CBHW080946170526
45158CB00008B/2392